"Rituals are so woven into our lives and into the universal order that it's easy to let them go unnoticed. Dru Johnson opens our eyes, not only to the presence of rites and rituals in all areas of life, but also to our need to be mindful of them. *Human Rites* is a compelling, challenging, and convicting read. We can't rid our lives of rituals (nor would we want to), but we can and should heed their value and power."

Karen Swallow Prior
author of *On Reading Well* and *Fierce Convictions*

"It's high time for the word 'ritual' to be redeemed and rediscovered for all of its potential, and Dru Johnson is the one to do it! He has distilled current research in ritual theory and biblical studies and has given us a creative exploration of how our rituals shape our lives and moral imaginations. Prepare to rethink everything you thought you knew about religious rituals!"

Tim Mackie
Co-creator of The Bible Project

"Human beings are creatures of habit, in particular, creatures of repetition and ritual. In this book, Dru Johnson shows us the importance of rituals, not just for life, but for the Christian life. Rituals give us scripts to follow to help us order our lives and to find meaning in a world that often appears mundane or overwhelming. Whether it is baptism or barbecue, Jewish Passover or a church potluck, Johnson shows you how extraordinary our ordinary feats of repetition turn out to be."

Michael F. Bird
Ridley College

"Whether consciously or unconsciously—whether actively or passively—we are all being formed by certain practices that we repeat again and again, also known as 'rituals' or 'rites.' Whatever our daily or seasonal rites may be, they have an effect on us as well as the world around us. In *Human Rites*, Dru helps us discern the difference be-

tween rites that are healthy and life-giving and those that are not challenging us to lean in to the former while forsaking the latter. As a constant work in process myself, I commend this helpful volume."

Scott Sauls
author of *Jesus Outside the Lines* and *Irresistible Faith*

"Delightful, insightful, and engaging from start to finish! Dru Johnson has given us a thoughtful and accessible introduction to the deeply powerful reality of habits and rites in every aspect of our lives. He concludes by offering an immensely practical template to help us grow in practical wisdom as ritualized creatures. Highly recommended!"

Jonathan T. Pennington
Southern Seminary

"Dru Johnson masterfully destroys the myth that following Jesus is a 'relationship, not a religion.' Not only do we learn how God blesses his people through traditions, rituals, liturgies, and religion; the book also teaches us why rituals matter to God and why they lead to spiritual thriving. This thought-provoking book teaches us to conform our everyday rituals to that which glorifies God. *Human Rites* is a game changer for the practice of Protestant Christianity."

Anthony Bradley
The King's College

"Dru Johnson writes that we are ritualed creatures who live in a ritualed world. We mark occasions by ritual 're-making of the ordinary' and learn to see and come to know through ritual performances. Johnson draws a crucial distinction between scripted rites and improvised rites. Of scripted rituals, he urges us to ask *who* is doing the scripting, and he explores what happens when rites go wrong, go flimsy, or go dark. This superb book is an accessible guide that will help us take our ritual inventory and learn to distinguish between the voice of the serpent and the voice of God."

Peter Leithart
Theopolis Institute

HUMAN RITES

The Power of Rituals, Habits, and Sacraments

Dru Johnson

WILLIAM B. EERDMANS PUBLISHING COMPANY
GRAND RAPIDS, MICHIGAN

Wm. B. Eerdmans Publishing Co.
4035 Park East Court SE, Grand Rapids, Michigan 49546
www.eerdmans.com

25 24 23 22 21 20 19   1 2 3 4 5 6 7

ISBN 978-0-8028-7600-3

Library of Congress Cataloging-in-Publication Data

A catalog record for this book is available from the Library of Congress.

To Stephanie,
my *first* wife in the Resurrection

Contents

Foreword

Kurt Vonnegut once dropped upon our species a maddeningly true statement: "We are what we pretend to be, so we must be careful about what we pretend to be."[1] This is very hard to argue with. Vonnegut, again, knows the score. This is indeed the drill. The world runs on pretense. We play along with the norms laid down by others, strengthening their power as we go, borrowing their plausibility in a lifelong bid to feel more plausible to ourselves and others. If we keep at it, maybe we'll finally feel too legit to quit, too credible to be denied, and, fingers crossed, worthy of a salaried position and a health-care plan. These are the exchanges that make our world turn. We become what we normalize, like it or not. But what if the norms according to which we lay down our lives as living sacrifices are unworthy of our best selves, our souls, or the possibility of real human thriving? What if they turn out to be wicked?

Into this very promising mess, Dru Johnson places before us the question of rituals. It turns out there's no escape from them. Even if we get free of one, we've really only ritualed our way into . . . wait for it . . . another, hopefully less toxic ritual, bound by

---

1. Kurt Vonnegut, introduction to *Mother Night* (New York: Dial Press, 2009), vi.

new bonds in a different deployment of energies. Human reality is made of rites done rightly and wrongly, knowingly and automatically, consciously and unconsciously. Rites are nonoptional.

What we do with our force of habit, Johnson argues, is what we do—and will have done—with our lives, the sum total of what we were up to. Getting our rites right is a very big deal—a life's work, in fact. What are we playing along with and why? If we delay or ignore this question, we may succeed in gaining a world of affirmation according to someone else's norms, but we risk forfeiting our soul, our *animus*, that interior part that still hungers and thirsts for the righteousness of God. In these pages, Johnson shows us how to begin the work of analyzing our own rituals (Who or what prescribed them? Are they worthy?) in the hope of living an undivided life.

This is an essential task in our radioactive days, days in which certain rituals seem almost designed to deaden our conscience, and rituals of deep attentiveness feel almost like a luxury our lives of high-tech haste can no longer afford. Most helpfully, Johnson wonders how it is that certain rituals become "dark and flimsy," tending toward estrangement, denial, and weakened spirit, and how we might bring them into the light so that our daily activities can support deep discernment, moral seriousness, and joy. In this, Johnson joins Henry David Thoreau as a voice that admonishes us against playing along with whatever it takes to avoid conflict and get by. Thoreau described the way his own conscience sometimes succumbed to such peer pressure thusly: "The greater part of what my neighbors call good I believe in my soul to be bad, and if I repent of anything, it is very likely to be my good behavior. What demon possessed me that I behaved so well?"[2]

We are, after all, what we abide. We emit what we admit. By inviting us to think through our own behaviors with deeper discern-

---

2. Henry David Thoreau, *Walden and the Famous Essay on "Civil Disobedience"* (New York: Signet, 1942), 12.

ment and a lively attentiveness to God's righteousness, Johnson invites us to consider, as prophetic thinking always does, the question of authority. What do righteous rites look like? How might our perverse designations give way to more beautiful orderings of our own energy expenditure from day to day? In considering these absolutely essential questions, Dru Johnson is a guide of deep wit, lyrical self-deprecation, and relentless wisdom.

DAVID DARK

Acknowledgments

Many thanks are due those who read bits and pieces of early versions: Judson Bliss, Anne Carman, Sharon Lindsay, Caroline Ratcliffe, and Aspen Scafa. Special thanks to Taylor Lindsay for her encouragement and comments on early drafts, but especially for gifting me with the arresting phrase "It's a ritual-eat-ritual world." This book springs from research I completed because of a generous grant from the John Templeton Foundation through Yoram Hazony and The Herzl Institute in 2013. Yoram's friendship has meant the world to me.

I wouldn't want to function in this world without Stephanie Johnson and our children: Claudia, Benjamin, Olivia, and Luisa (in no particular order). Equally, the academic world would suck the life out of me without colleagues such as Josh Blander, Anthony Bradley, Eric Bennett, Ryan O'Dowd, Jonathan Pennington, Michael Rhodes, Jennifer Tharp, Gregory Thornbury, and just about everyone at The King's College, *especially my students* (not to mention regular help from Kimberly Thornbury, Rebecca Au-Mullaney, and Natalie Nakamura). Thank you to our crew at Pennington Court and Comunidade Cristã Presbiteriana church in Newark, New Jersey, for helping our family to practice the good news. (Looking at you, Kezia Paschoal!)

I wouldn't have had the courage to write this book without the editorial coaching of Lil Copan, who made it happen. Brutal honesty is my love language, and Lil is fluent. And I would be even more embarrassed about the writing within it apart from the editorial savvy of Mary Hietbrink. *Nota bene*: So many of these thoughts merely wax *ritual-ly* on what I have learned from Esther Meek over the last two decades.

Know Your Rites

What did you have for breakfast?

Really—what was it?

How did you prepare it?

Do you make the same meal over and over every morning?

At what point did your routine breakfast become a morning ritual?

When we go to the doctor, they may ask us what we had for breakfast. Sometimes to test our memory after we've gotten a bump on the head, other times to figure out our version of a healthy diet. Doctors who see dozens of patients a day have rituals they've created from routines, but also scripted rituals that they were taught in medical school, like asking what we had for breakfast. At some point, routines cross a magical line to become rituals. And sometimes those are rituals we teach and share with others.

If you've taught your children how to do their own laundry, you likely taught them *your particular ritual for laundering clothes.* Yours isn't the only way, but it's a way that works.

If we're being attentive to our lives, we might ask how much of what we do throughout the day consists of rites grown out of our routines (like laundry), and how much consists of what we've been taught (like medical skills). We might ask why we're doing those rites, who creates the ritual scripts that we perform, or what the goal of our rituals is.

Some of us wait until life has broken down before examining our ritualed world. But others of us want to understand our rituals now. When we do, we discover ways to foster and sustain good ritualed lives, lives aimed at discernment and flourishing.

When I undertook this exercise in understanding, I saw everything I did in a different light. Kissing my wife good-bye every morning took on new meaning when I realized it was a rite with a goal. Morning workouts became intellectual journeys. I could see how my pre-programmed reactions to the triumphs and foolishness of my kids held them captive and became a grid through which we all processed the world. When I realized how my embodied life shaped me intellectually, emotionally, and communally, I re-evaluated everything I did with my body—which means exactly that: I re-evaluated everything I did, every ritual.

No longer did I see my actions as neutral. They either pointed me to a better understanding of the world or blinded me to it. As a spouse, parent, former pastor, and now professor, I also realized that I hand out rites left and, well, right. As a parent I say, "Stay at the table for dinnertime." "We're turning off electronics for two hours." And my favorite, "Let's just stare out the windows on this drive." We're all performing rituals according to scripts handed to us or fashioned by us and asking others to do the same.

Whether serving in the military or adjusting to retirement, whether dressing kids or being assisted with a disability, whether living in a "McMansion" or public housing, we all find meaning in and through our rituals. In these pages I hope you'll join me to pause and reflect on whose rituals we're embodying and why.

One of my earliest and deepest understandings of ritual came at warp speed when I joined the military. No matter what branch of the military new recruits join, they share similar experiences from the first night of boot camp. For me and my troop, it was being up for long night hours, standing in lines, looking ridiculous in civilian clothes. Being swarmed by sergeants roaring at us, their faces just inches from ours. The brims of their Smokey-the-Bear hats poking us in the forehead as their shouts mixed commands with insults.

According to them, we did everything incorrectly. In the July-hot night of San Antonio, Texas, they told us that we had picked up our luggage the wrong way. So they made us set our bags down and pick them back up hundreds of times until we could do it *just so.*

Sometime after three a.m., we collapsed in our bunks. Most of us didn't know what to make of the evening's events. I was just seventeen, confused and exhausted. I fell asleep in a room full of strangers.

Then came the terrifying part. Between sleeping and waking, I heard a drill sergeant banging on the door to the barracks, screaming at the night guard. (That guard was just another puke like me. We all pulled guard duty in the barracks. And when God hated us most, he sent screaming drill sergeants to test the duty of our guard at zero four hundred hours.)

In his best bulldog voice, he barked through the door, "IF YOU DON'T OPEN THIS DOOR RIGHT NOW, I AM GOING TO TEAR YOUR HEAD OFF AND DO UNSPEAKABLE THINGS TO YOU!"

It was as if they'd released a frothing wild dog into our barracks. Sure enough, a metal trashcan came flying down the center aisle, clanging against the metal bunks on which we now pretended to sleep. "UP, YOU MAGGOTS!" More drill sergeants came in to pile on the fun and harass anything that moved. I still consider boot camp the worst kind of waking up there is. If you want more details, ask a veteran. He or she can tell you loads of stories filled with anxiety and excitement and boredom.

When I woke up to find this well-dressed, screaming bulldog on the loose in our barracks, one thought came to my mind:

"WHY DID I DO THIS?" This wasn't fun, and I truly didn't understand why I felt that way. I loved war movies. I must have watched Stanley Kubrick's *Full Metal Jacket* a dozen times. The first half of the movie portrays a no-holds-barred version of Marine Corps boot camp. I couldn't get enough of it.

Yet, when the sergeants were yelling directly *at me*, I hated it. And it never became fun. (The military has strict orders to vacuum out ahead of time anything that might possibly be or become fun in its procedures.) Everything had to be done *just so*. Failure to do it *just so* reaped inordinately harsh consequences: yelling, push-ups, cleaning duty, more yelling, and so on. My father's stories of Army basic training teemed with fun, and they were fun to listen to—maybe because the drill sergeants he described yelled at him and not me.

I didn't want their rituals. It turns out that I just wanted all the trappings of the military life without any of the embodied processes required to appreciate them.

On that first night, I just wanted to quit. And that terrified me. How could I be so easily swayed from my lifetime obsession with the military by one night's experience?

Why am I telling you this? Because basic military training may be one of the most ritualized experiences in the world. It blows religious rituals out of the water in terms of meticulous performances. The military scripts and choreographs everything so that it's done *just so*: picking up a fork in the chow hall, folding underwear with tweezers and a ruler, marching in exact synchronicity, and on and on.

Though we all hated it at the time, most of us look back now and talk about boot camp as a religious experience. And I found out that my dad hated boot camp too. But he talked about it all the time when I was a kid. His military stories cropped up most readily when we kids were whining about doing something difficult. You could almost hear the "back in my day" engine winding up.

(For what it's worth, I do exactly the same thing to my children today.)

My fellow recruits and I could moan all we wanted, but in that short time in boot camp we didn't just learn—we became different sorts of human beings. We couldn't conceive that surmounting many of those challenges was even possible. We didn't know we could march *that* precisely, stand *that* long in the sun, walk *that* far, or get all sixty of us teenagers showered and shaved in under twenty minutes.

Uncle Sam had specific purposes for all of those studiously ritualized details in our walking, eating, standing, sleeping, folding, cleaning, and more. Many of us were going to carry loaded weapons or fix avionics on aircraft. If we couldn't clean a toilet bowl to standards, then how could we be trusted with live ammunition or a pilot's life?

All of those rituals had an invisible arrow running through them that pointed toward a goal. Although we didn't know it at the time, every ritual of boot camp aimed at a greater purpose. Our drill sergeants were trying to teach us many things in a compressed amount of time. It didn't matter that we couldn't figure out why we had to fold our underwear into four-inch squares. We had to trust them and fully commit ourselves to all the strange rituals they demanded of us.

The result: boot camp changed the way I see myself, my community, and the world. It was the closest thing I'd known to a religious experience at that point in my life. Even in the middle of it, I knew I would never be the same. (And a friendly note to the reader: Don't worry—this book won't be a bunch of stories from the military. Just two.)

When I later worked as a pastor, I was surprised to find out that rituals and religious experiences didn't belong solely to the territory of the church. Lots of people say similar things about attending university, being pregnant, battling addiction, giving birth, deteriorating through cancer, adopting, marrying, divorcing, and other life events. Some of these rituals, like marriage, we embody wholeheartedly. Others happen to us, by choice or against our will, and rituals sprout from them, like funerals.

In fact, rituals are so foundational to our lives and society that it's ironic how negative we have become towards them. Even learning rote rituals can help us think more clearly or save our lives. After dozens of ritual attempts, when an M-16 rifle jammed, I could strip it apart and get it working again by rote. When I was in a foxhole preparing for an attack, I literally saw my relationship with my rifle differently because I knew *by rote memory* what to do in case of malfunction. And if you don't know, the M-16 likes its malfunctions. (That was the last military example. I promise.)

OK, so most of us aren't in a foxhole with a junky M-16. (Thank God!) But let's consider some good reasons why rote rituals help us to better understand the world. Most of us were taught basic mathematics through the rote rituals of times tables. Because I don't need to grapple with what 3×7 equals—which I ritually memorized in elementary school—I can focus my mathematical thinking on more complex problems. Similarly, many of us have memorized a number of formulaic prayers. Although these can sometimes seem stale and meaningless, knowing prayers by rote can free us to think through the words and focus on the God we petition or praise.

It's not quite right to say that rituals surround us. Instead, we are *ritualed* creatures, designed to understand everything from microbiology to statistical models to the emotions of others through ritual performance. A musician can know a song, a nurse can know a heartbeat isn't quite right on an EKG, and we all can know $3 \times 7 = 21$ because we've participated in rituals that allowed us to understand these things.

In this book I want to explore with you the way in which rituals become meaningful. That might include not knowing exactly how rituals work or what they mean when we first start doing them.

But in these pages, I hope that we can figure out together why we perform the rituals that already pervade our lives.

One thing's for sure: after I had spent years of thinking about the rituals of math, boot camp, medical school, parenting, and more, my views had to change. Now, whenever I meet someone who is wise, I wonder: *Whose rituals did she embody to become so discerning?* All of us follow certain people down a ritual trail, and it's essential to discern our ritual sources and the paths we choose.

Standing in front of the wall-sized canvas at the Metropolitan Museum in New York, visitors react in one of two ways.

"A kid could have painted this!"

"Wow! This is an actual Jackson Pollock."

After brief exposure to the "classics" of modern art, many of us have probably slipped into the first reaction. We stare at the piece and search, longing to discover some pattern hidden in it. In drips and splatters of earth-toned paints, we scan for any signs of "autumn" or "rhythm" in Pollock's *Autumn Rhythm*. The painting leaves us overwhelmed with impressions and reactions, but yields no discernible message, story, or image of ourselves.

Then, we come across an essay, or maybe an explainer video, revealing this piece of art to us. It turns out that most modern artists were classically trained painters.[1] They were fully capable of painting like Rembrandt, but they chose to do something different instead.

To us amateurs, such works look simple and lazy. Yet, experts who look at these pieces of art will point out the subtle distinguishing details—like the paint strokes that are actually difficult to make—which reveal that trained artists must have produced such works.

The community of experts who can distinguish a child's smudges from a master artist's canvas hears this claim repeatedly.

---

1. The PBS explainer video "I Could Do That" is an excellent example: https://www.youtube.com/watch?v=67EKAIY43kg.

They respond to "I could do that" with "No, you couldn't. And, more importantly, you didn't do it." Meaning that it looks easy only to the untrained eye and unskilled hand. Art is a complex response *to* and powerful shaper *of* culture, which explains why it wasn't you or I who created that piece of art. We weren't there, we weren't involved in that cultural moment, and we weren't skilled enough to make it look that easy.

After taking an art history course and visiting museums with experts, hardly anyone would persist in arguing, "My kid could have done that" (unless their names were Mr. and Mrs. Pollock). Experts who can see the same painting differently are like guides through the jungle. Guides can see paths through dense undergrowth, paths indiscernible to those without skilled understanding.

Today I can no longer fool myself into believing that I cut my own trail into the world. I need people with expertise, guides with wisdom ritualized into them that enables them to see what I cannot. Of this I'm confident: If our bodily practices determine how we understand the world, then we might want to ask ourselves these important questions: Who is offering us the rituals we practice? By what authority? And to what end?

The ritualed world I'm describing isn't an equal world. We bear different perspectives shaped by different ritual experiences, which should enrich our communities in the best of circumstances. Some are teachers while others are students. Some give Communion while others receive; the same goes for prayer. Rituals of elite athletes are off-limits to people with basic athletic skills. Birthing rituals—well, you get the idea. They're different depending on who you are in the relationship. Our body, our subculture, our position in life, our race, our experiences, and more will shape the rituals we perform.

Some rituals cut across cultures, but those who've lived internationally know that many do not. Within American culture, white folks can be easily offended by meal rituals in black-American or Puerto Rican-American culture (and vice versa). The waste disposal rituals of some American Christians stupefy many European Christians, who see tending the earth as a biblical duty. Because we don't all get equal access to rituals, we bring all kinds of culturally loaded ideas about rites to the table. But our diverse participation in rituals isn't necessarily a bad thing. The diversity in our experiences allows us to consider what people do and why, and can help us avoid discussing rituals that are new to us in a judgmental way. My goal is to help us appreciate how rituals shape our understanding and know how to discern when rituals go bad—both in the humdrum of daily life and in the sacraments of the church.

Our entire world—our faith traditions, professions, cultures, and embodied lives—is shot through with ritual. My hope is that I can share tools that will enable us to answer questions like these:

- Which rituals do we already embody?
- Why do we practice those rites and not others?
- Who or what prescribes these rituals to us?
- Should we change them (and if so, then how)?

Until we begin to see how thoroughly ritualed our world is, we won't ask the rite questions. Until something has gone wrong with our rites, we won't feel the implications of our rituals. When this happens, it may unsettle us, but it shouldn't discourage us from trying to make our rites right. My goal is to work with you to do just that. Ultimately, this book is an attempt to build a ritual toolbox with you, aimed to suit you and your community and your ability to thrive together. And this book, like all books, comes with a ritual built in. Now, we must perform it.

OUR RITUALED WORLD

Chapter 1

More than Mind Games

We are shaped by our tools.

Sherry Turkle, *Alone Together*

When many of us hear the word "ritual," we think of religion or mindless behaviors (or both). Whatever rituals are, can we honestly reduce them to religious tools? In order to grasp hold of our ritualed world, we must first grasp who or what is writing our rites and understand why they want us to perform their rituals. Neglecting the source of our rituals is dangerous—naïve at best. In order to see this, we need to think first about button-pushing and pill-swallowing—of course!

Prepare yourself. The following paragraphs may be difficult to accept.

The best estimates claim that 80 percent of the "Close Door" buttons on New York City elevators don't work. They're busted by design.[1] Either they were never wired to the elevator in the first place, or, after breaking, they were never repaired. Why? Most likely, it's because it doesn't really matter if the "Close Door" buttons actually work.

1. http://www.radiolab.org/story/buttons-not-buttons/.

By the time we become impatient enough to search out the "Close Door" button and push it, sometimes repeatedly, the control system shuts the doors automatically, regardless of what we do. So we push the button, and soon after, the doors close, and we feel like we've taken control. But our anxious taps on a defunct button have not interfered with the control of the elevator. For this reason, those in the know call these "placebo buttons." These are hard truths indeed. Take a moment if you need it, because now it becomes harder.

Studies of placebo pills have uncovered startling evidence of their effectiveness. It turns out that those placebos, which are just harmless sugar pills, might be one of the most successful drug therapies in medicine. That's right. If a patient merely believed that a sugar pill acted as a drug targeted at her sickness, then actual symptoms sometimes responded in kind. Researchers thought that this effect was due to mind over matter: If I believe the pill helps me, then my body will make itself better.

Because of these consistent findings, research expanded to include other kinds of placebo treatments. Patients were now told the pill was, in fact, a placebo. Doctors instructed patients to take the pill as if it were a real medicine. To the surprise of most, it still worked sometimes. People got better even when they knew the treatment wasn't real.

What caused the placebo effect when the ruse of the placebo was exposed from the outset? Further studies indicated that several factors played a role.

When a doctor did three things, the effectiveness of the placebo increased. She asked personal questions displaying care for the patient *apart from the current illness*. She showed confidence in her diagnosis. And she prescribed a placebo to be taken in a specific regimen. If the doctor cared, knew what to do, and prescribed a clear ritual—"Take this pill three times a day and only after a full glass of cold water"—placebos still worked even when the patient knew it was a sugar pill.

What's going on here? Taking the sugar pill as the doctor directed appears to develop into a ritual for the patient. This ritual doesn't presume that the sugar pill will heal the patient. Instead, the patient performs an action that directly represents the relationship with the physician. Swallowing the sugar pill is the sacrament—as it were—that demonstrates her trust in the doctor.

Somehow—and nobody currently knows how—participating in that whole ritual process of going to the doctor, being given personal care and a confident diagnosis, being prescribed a particular treatment, and performing the pill-taking ritual changes the physiology of the sick patient.

I warned you. These truths are hard to swallow.

Rituals Inside and Out

Though rituals often get type-cast in religious roles, they make regular cameos elsewhere in our lives. Think about this with me: How many of our activities could be described as rituals without a relationship to religion? Here's just a short list:

Checking social media
Having family dinner together
Driving home from work
Setting up holiday decorations
Meeting a friend in a pub
Tucking children into bed
Packing for vacation
Calling our parents
Preparing to speak in public

How many of these do we act out devoutly, embodying similar routines almost every time? Maybe more of our life is ritualed than we tend to think.

And if that's true, what do rituals do for us? For instance, is baptism like the "Close Door" button on the elevator: a trick of the cruel world that does nothing more than make us feel as if we have some control?

Or are rituals more like swallowing sugar pills when we know that they're just that—showy performances with blind hope? Are religious rituals simply acts meant to show our trust in a caring God, even though we know that the rituals themselves do nothing for us?

Some have even suggested that rituals symbolically express our internal thoughts. Just as poetry or music can give emotional shape to our thoughts, rituals symbolically encode our deepest thoughts and storylines into performances.

Growing up in the late twentieth century, I certainly believed my inner thought-life, the part of myself that I could hide from others, represented the *real* me. Most of my outward behaviors were just a show. Deep down inside, where no one else could see—that's where you'd find the real me, along with my authentic beliefs.

It's a popular way to think of ourselves: the *real* me hides inside, and I show the world the "pretend" me. This view of ourselves comes out when our body language doesn't match our spoken words. Our non-verbal cues betray our inner thoughts, so they say.

According to this view, we outwardly express our inner thoughts when we create rituals. For instance, if we're convinced that harmful germs are everywhere, our bodily practices reflect our inward convictions. We repetitively wash our hands, use hand sanitizer, avoid touching public surfaces, and the like. (I feel compelled to add that, like everything else, "germs" can be both helpful and harmful to us.)

Our rituals represent an embodied parable based on our story of the world. Our body is the stage, and our ritual movements perform as actors. If this is correct, then to understand our thoughts, we simply decode the symbols of our outward actions. Staring at the floor *equals* shame. Lowering our head in prayer *equals* reverence. All three views sketched above seem to have some truth to them. Like pushing the elevator button, enacting rites seems to do something for us. Like taking a prescribed pill, following rites requires our trusting participation in order to be effective. Like a stage performance, our ritual actions outwardly reveal our thought-lives in some way. But none of these views allows us to fully understand ritual. For instance, it's difficult to see someone kneeling in tears and not immediately try to decode what's going on in their inner thoughts. But what is it? Are they distraught? Overjoyed? Or are they attempting to display submission to God? Or maybe it's something else. . . .

My old assumption—that my rituals symbolically revealed my thought life to the watching world—can't adequately explain the kneeling person in tears. The longer I lived, the more I came to realize that rites also do something *to* me.

As anthropologist Catherine Bell said, "Kneeling does not merely *communicate* subordination [to outside observers]. . . . For all intents and purposes, kneeling produces a subordinated kneeler in and through the act itself."[2] So, not only can my outward actions express my inner thoughts, but my bodily actions can shape them too! Influence flows both ways! The world of my thoughts interacts dynamically with the world of my actions. And I see the world differently. In fact, because of rituals, we all do.

Consider the rituals of parenting an infant. From the feeding regimen to the midnight diaper changes, all of the rituals that emerge from parenting transform the way we see the same places we've always been. For most of us, the world looks different. We now comprehend humans in their most fragile state. Because of this, every coffee table's edge appears more jagged, every public

2. Catherine Bell, *Ritual Theory, Ritual Practice* (New York: Oxford University Press, 2009), 100.

handrail more filthy, and every stranger's sneeze more menacing than before. The embodied practices of parenting infants rearrange our interior mental life, our outward behavior, and our perceptions.

Notice that we've started thinking about two different types of rituals:

- Rituals that are taught through traditions (to which we'll return)
- Rituals that emerge from daily practices

This is key as we think more about our ritualed lives. In both cases, rituals turn on *who* or *what* is teaching us the rites. In some cases, religion, colleagues, parents, or others teach us rituals. Some call these rituals "traditions." In other cases, just functioning as humans in the real world itself will generate rituals, such as those behaviors generated by driving a car.

Religious Rituals?

A third category of rites fits in here somewhere, though I'm not sure exactly what we should call them. Prescribed by God and shared through the prophets, these rituals get set apart from tradition-taught rituals because of their divine origins.

If there is a God who created the universe, and if that God has adequately instructed us in how to exist in the world, prophetically given rituals form a distinct set of rites. In some ways, these God-given rites will be similar to the rituals of learning engine repair and getting ready for bed. But they take priority in our understanding of our ritualed world, primarily because they might reveal something about the way we were created to exist in it.

In all cases, whether we like it or not, rites are forging us. We might listen to cultural and institutional voices, often uncritically embodying the rites they prescribe. Our workplace peers, the podcasts we listen to, our profession's marks of success, the expectations of our parents, clothing ads, our smartphones, and dozens of other voices whisper (and sometimes shout), constantly attempting to get us to embody their ritual practices.

Because ours is a *ritualed world*, it's important for us to think about how rites shape us. After all, intentionally embracing valid rituals can shape us for good, but uncritically embodying rituals handed down from dubious voices cannot end well.

This is the exact crux that the Hebrew Scriptures highlight: the serpent's voice in the Garden of Eden was dubious, as attested by God's only question of the man: "Who told you that you were naked?" Voices will script rites for us: "When you eat of it, you will be like God, knowing good and evil." And we will come to know the world one way or the other: "Their eyes were opened, and they knew that they were naked." Scripture presses us to listen to the voice of God, who scripts for us an embodied life in order for us to see what he is showing us and to share that wisdom with others. And if God created us as ritualed humans, then our exploration of rites can't be limited to religion. If we are indeed shaped by our rituals, it includes everything.

Chapter 2

Guided by Voices

You're gonna have to serve somebody.

Bob Dylan, "Gotta Serve Somebody"

For anthropologists, rituals are ordinary human practices strategically changed and improvised for another purpose. This definition seems to answer the question "What is a ritual?" But it really doesn't. It shifts the question from a "what" to a "who": Who is strategically changing what, and for what purpose?

Baptism changes the normal practice of water cleansing to a form of initiation. Christians have improvised the ritual of baptism by dunking, pouring, or sprinkling with water because the New Testament gives few details about how to baptize.

The Lord's Supper takes an ordinary human meal and strategically changes it into a meal specifically for understanding Jesus's death and resurrection. Technically, the meal was already strategically changed into a ritual—the Israelite Passover meal—when Jesus re-ritualized it into Communion the night prior to his crucifixion. It's that "strategically changed" bit that begs all sorts of questions. Who gets to change practices into rites? What's their strategy? Who authorized them?

Christian Scripture speaks about rituals without saying how to perform them—rites such as fasting, meditating, praying, worshiping, and getting married appear in Scripture without a real script, leaving us holding the bag full of improvisations.

White Weddings

On that list of rituals without detailed script is the wedding. Who needs this ritual, exactly? When a couple asked me (as a newly ordained minister) to perform my first wedding ceremony, I went to Scripture for guidance. When I had reduced myself to embarrassing word searches, I realized that I couldn't find the passages outlining wedding ceremonies in Scripture.

As a recent seminary graduate, I sheepishly admitted to myself that I needed guidance. I asked the senior pastor for help in finding those texts. That's when I first learned the dark secret about Christian weddings: we've made them up. Or, put more diplomatically, weddings are improvised rituals.

The Bible describes weddings with almost no detail. Genesis barely even recorded the first marriage of the man and woman in Eden. Jacob's bamboozled wedding to Leah implies only that their honeymoon night required sex in a tent. (When we remember that Jacob comes from nomadic stock, we realize that sex in a tent wasn't so exotic for them.)

The Bible leaves us with all kinds of unanswered questions. Did a couple recite vows and punctuate them with "I do's"? Did a priest pronounce them husband and wife? Strange as it may seem, the biblical authors don't say much about one of humankind's most significant life events. Even stranger, the Hebrew and Christian Scriptures say so much about other rituals that seem less pertinent. (The Torah spends lots of time telling people how to be ritually clean after having sex, how to responsibly own an ox, and what to do after killing a man in battle.)

At weddings today, we participate in a flurry of modern rituals shaped mostly by our culture. Visualize in your mind the last big wedding you attended. Then ask yourself how many of the things happening in that wedding reflected teachings in Scripture. Next, ask yourself how many of those things took ordinary activities from your culture and strategically changed them for this purpose?

Our weddings often include florally spruced churches, a white dress donned for this day only, exchanged rings, embellished and impractical vows sworn, clerical powers invoked, and processional walking. When the proceedings begin, Pachelbel's *Canon in D* delicately guides the participants into their ceremonial pigeonholes.

Incidentally, my wife and I sometimes discuss what we would have done differently in our own wedding. We would have made it simpler, maybe even smaller. In other words, we would have let the 1990s American wedding culture have less influence on our ceremony.

Why all the fanfare and flourish in our weddings?

When one couple asked me what had to happen in their wedding in order for them to be married, I told them the dirty little secret. As the officiate, I could simply ask them, "Do you agree to be married?," and if they both said "Yes," they would be just as married as any other husband and wife in our state.

Even so, we do recognize weddings as a special circumstance—even elopements, when couples get married at the courthouse. This tells us something about the role of ritual in our lives.

But what exactly makes a wedding a type of ritual?

The answer should sound familiar by now: *Every element of a wedding is something taken from ordinary life and then exaggerated for a purpose*. It's not unusual to put on a dress, to wear a ring, to make promises, or to walk to meet someone. But in a wedding, every ordinary thing is made special and given a new significance. The dress is festooned. Participants walk with slow, measured steps. The promises are overstated. (After all, who actually keeps all of their wedding vows on any given day of their marriage?) The rings are dedicated to wear on a specific finger. Wedding culture strategically re-makes ordinary objects and activities into rituals for this day only. This *re-making of the ordinary* tells us something about what people think marriage is.

And though the Bible gives no instructions on how to get married, we ritualize our weddings anyway. And because we improvise upon the veritable silence of Scripture, our weddings divulge what our culture acclaims as much as what a marriage is about. Let's get real: these days, Pinterest plans more elements of the wedding than the pastor does. In the end, our improvisations reveal our traditions and show what we think must be done in order to properly inaugurate a lifelong monogamous relationship.

Other Rites on Demand

Improvised rituals don't emerge only from daily routines. Nor must an authority explicitly prescribe these rituals in detail. We improvise in response to demands for ritual in our lives: for days that we hold sacred, milestones, achievements, and more. The most obvious rituals in Scripture that require improvisation are the marriage ceremony and the practice of Sabbath rest. Both occur in the creation narratives without any specific instructions. And even when a ritual's instructions are given, as with the Lord's Supper, improvisation is still required to some extent.

Consider the performances involved in all the different rituals of our lives. Closing on a house mortgage basically involves sitting at a table and enduring the request to sign a mountain of documents. It's like some bizarre form of celebrity. You repeatedly give your autograph in order to indenture yourself to your sole obsessive fan: the bank. The ordinary act of signing your name is elevated because it's being done for a special purpose. And the bank requires *many signatures* in *many places*—and all of them require the signatures of witnesses!

We celebrate birthdays with the ordinary practice of eating food—but not just any food: It's the favorite meal of the person being celebrated. Birthday cakes are just a dessert, but strategically re-made for the rite with lots of frosting and candles.

We create special rituals around significant events such as adopting a child, going away to school, and grieving for the recently deceased. On the most momentous occasions of life, we find ourselves improvising rituals handed to us from our culture and our religious traditions. But those aren't necessarily dictated from Scripture, and so we improvise faithfully.

Ritual pervades the performances of our everyday lives as well. Getting the kids ready for school becomes a "daily ritual." Patterns emerge from our lives so naturally that we can be easily understood when we talk about "bathroom rituals," or the ritual of preparing a parent's daily medications, or the rite of getting coffee with a friend.

In all of these rituals, we change, exaggerate, or refocus ordinary human activities in order to do something that cannot be done otherwise. In the process, we shape and form the people who participate in the ritual. And now we can't help but notice that all rituals originate from the world of everyday objects and practices.

Our initial question incorrectly assumed that rituals could be described as a "what" (What *are* rituals?). In the end, rituals have as much to do with who prescribes them as what they ask us to do. Because rites betray strategic thinking, we need to know whose ritual voice we "serve" as well as their ritual goals for us.

The Call to a Ritualed Life

Our world breathes with ritual. As we examine our ritualed world together, we can also think about how we might embody the rites of our daily lives in light of Christian mandates.

Jesus didn't call people to take up their *minds* and follow him; he prescribed an embodied life of rituals as a sort of classroom for early followers. Communion and baptism form just one aspect of the embodied rituals that shape Jesus's instruction to his disciples. In ritualizing a life for them, he carries forward the same impulse of the Torah. The sacraments of the disciples' Scripture also taught Israel, from the time of Egyptian slavery up to first-century Galilee, shaping them to see the world differently.

Notice that the Torah's central rituals—Sabbath, Passover, Pentecost, the Day of Atonement, and the Feast of Booths—all focus Israel's attention on understanding their own history *through those rituals* in order to understand God's current instruction to them. It's important to note that they couldn't understand their own history properly without embodying those rites of the Torah.

The Torah re-makes all kinds of ordinary activities into rituals for the sake of knowing, for helping God's people see something that God is showing them. Yes, those rituals certainly contain symbols and express something about their views of God and self. But Israel is instructed by God to perform rites in order to *know*.

The ultimate goal is not to perform the ritual, *but to see what is being shown.* Consider a medical student who ritually studies x-rays under the guidance of a radiology professor. Without the ritual of learning to read x-rays, she will never see the things the professor is trying to show her. An x-ray might fascinate the eyes, but the uninterpreted x-ray is impenetrable and useless as a medical tool.

As I see it, the Scriptures portray Israel and the church as the students of God, embodying the directions in order to see what God is showing us. If that's correct, then it's possible that without practicing those New Testament rituals, we won't know what God intends to show us.

Whether we like it or not, someone or something always scripts our ritualed lives, and Scripture wants to play a formative role in our practices. This requires us to know what kind of ritualed world the biblical authors present to us. If we can hear their voices, we can also critically engage the rites handed to us from our traditions and our culture.

The Voices

Whether or not we are conscious of them, we live out rituals scripted by our societal orbits. "It may be the devil . . . or the Lord, but you're gonna have to serve somebody," as Bob Dylan says. Often we find ourselves uncritically following the cultural voices that commend our practices by fiat. All of our lives, they've whispered to us suggestively, "Do this to be that." Many of us have listened and behaved according to that script.

Think with me about some examples. To be more attractive, we trustingly embody fitness and clothing regimens prescribed by health and beauty magazines. You may imagine different clothing and exercise rites than I do, but you certainly think of *something*, and that image comes from *somewhere* in our culture.

Out of a desire for the trappings of Western education, we commit ourselves to the rites of university performance (with the best of intentions)—listening to lectures, reading books, writing essays, and receiving critiques—in order for those ineffable processes to yield insight and discernment.

In order to project stories about ourselves to others, we pay good money for clothes, makeup, and scarification rituals. We dress and groom ourselves carefully. And we scar tattoos into our appendages in an effort to capture our culture's respect—as cool, hip, what have you—in all its evanescence. We've been ritualized to use media tools to propagate our curated images of the life we've always longed for. But who is scripting these rites, and to what end?

Against the grain of cultural rites that promise the ability to shape our world according to our curated tastes, the biblical prophets insist that it is *we who must be shaped* by Scripture's guidance first. That process of being shaped by Scripture's voice and improvising Scripture's rituals produces wisdom. And wisdom remains the gold standard of humanity as far as Scripture is concerned.

The biblical authors seem convinced that our understanding of the cosmos is shaped by our ritual practices. We can listlessly float along in a sea of inherited rituals, or we can become discerning practitioners of the rites that shape our vision of reality, of God, and of self.

As we come to appreciate good and beautiful aspects in our rites, we will need to be able to discern what good rites are and how even good rites can be twisted for ill. This inevitably begins with an assessment of the voices we listen to and the scripts we follow.

The voices commended here come from ancient biblical prophets and from Jesus with his apostles—people keen on forging discernment within the cultures in which they lived. However, many periods of our lives aren't scripted. So what rituals emerge from such moments of scriptlessness?

Our Ritual Guides

Chapter 3

Priestly Monkeys Banging on
Their Ritual Typewriters

I found that the stuff that I'd been really embarrassed of at
the time when I was in my early 20s . . . [was] *not knowing
anything and just this feeling of scriptlessness* that one has when
one is younger.

Elif Batuman, *Fresh Air* interview, NPR

"Tell me! I don't know how you saw the thing so clear. What
should I do?"

Adam, in John Steinbeck, *East of Eden*

You shall dwell in shelters for seven days. All native Israelites shall live in shelters, in order that your generations may
know that I made the people of Israel dwell in shelters when I
brought them out of the land of Egypt: I am Yahweh your God.

Leviticus 23:42–43

At some point in our lives, the scripts handed to us from significant adults and peers disintegrate. If we're starting out on our
own, we may decide we no longer subscribe to the rites of our
family's vacation or the rituals of university education. And we
don't know what to do. Until that moment, we didn't realize

how much work these well-worn paths did for us—how much comfort they provided, how much rest. Elif Batumen (quoted above) nails that sense of aimlessness we've all known. Whether we're in our twenties or further on in life, that "feeling of scriptlessness" and the embarrassment that comes with it can take us captive.

Scriptlessness can feel like a forest of proliferating paths forward, with no maps. What we experience isn't quite listlessness or discontent; it's either not knowing what to do or feeling saturated with too many options. And they can't all be correct.

All of us will be confronted with circumstances that leave us breathless and scriptless. Sometimes these circumstances are sudden and intrusive; other times they're creeping and inevitable. Akin to being dropped into the thick of the jungle, scriptlessness envelops us, and no clear route emerges, no path to chop or trudge. Scriptless periods of life engulf us, our friends, parishioners, students, and families when life changes:

> When our parents' strict rules faded as we went off to the libertine structures and loose morals of college.
> When my husband and I divorced.
> When we buried our child.
> When "the church" widened into a more diverse collection of people and beliefs than our individual church experiences allowed us to understand.
> When our friend confessed an inappropriate sexual dalliance to us.

At these junctures in life, we often sputter and spew out the rituals that we've tacitly absorbed through culture. As a teacher, I've overheard young adults coaching their peers through rough patches with rituals gleaned from *Sex and the City*. A young man struggling with rejection once informed me, "My roommates said I should drown myself in video games for a few days" (as if that was the prudish form of drinking away his sorrows). Essentially, they prescribed a ritual for him.

I asked him, "Have your roommates experienced this problem before? Have they struggled through it? Do they know its implications ten years from now? If not, then why are you listening to them? Have you thought about using Ben & Jerry's instead?" So I replaced one suggested ritual with another. Let's face it—we've all done this to ourselves or others.

Because scriptlessness has universal features, good novels can examine and illuminate the need for guides who can script a way forward. *East of Eden,* the novel by John Steinbeck, masters the scriptless narrative arc. His characters and plots feature honest-to-God folks, people I've known and stories in which I myself have drowned.

In this novel, Steinbeck's main character, Adam, marries in haste and ignores the looming tsunami of predicaments he's walked himself into. Steinbeck showcases Adam's weaknesses best when Adam loses all sense of direction, when he can find no script.

Halfway through the novel, Adam's ideas regarding a pre-formatted route to happiness are torn apart. He discovers that his wife is actually an icy-hearted anti-saint—red in tooth and claw. Life clarifies this when his wife communicates with him through the cold steel of his .45 caliber six-shooter. She heats it up with one lead bullet and puts that round right through his shoulder. On her way out the door, she quietly steps over her poor, bleeding Adam, abandoning him, his garden, and her two young children. Brutal!

What happens when the script fails us? In Adam's case, he twists himself into a psychological coma during the next several months. He slumps around in his scriptlessness, fruitlessly sorting through questions about what went wrong. Alone with the slow corrosion of his thoughts, he neglects his home, his garden, and his two young sons.

Eventually, his ever-wise blacksmith physically breaks Adam out of his stupor. Samuel the smithy slaps the listless Adam around and forces him to face the ruin of his life. Adam clenches his fists in begrudging response:

> "You make me doubt myself," Adam said fiercely. "You always have. I'm afraid of you. What should I do, Samuel? Tell me! I don't know how you saw the thing so clear. What should I do?"[1]

Samuel sees a clear path through the riot of Adam's hapless thoughts. He ably guides Adam out, scripting a way forward for him. He drags Adam to the trailhead and makes him walk, even against Adam's will at points.

In the moments of our worst crises, most of us don't know what to do. We can't make out a pattern to our pain or see a path through the dizzying overgrowth of our torments.

At times like these, pretenders may enter the scene as well, sometimes seeking to manipulate us. But the harmful ignorance of e'er-do-well friends can wreak equal havoc. When we're fighting our way through the fog of poor advice, why don't we follow Adam and let more experienced folk guide us?

Not many of us will have our spouse put a bullet in our shoulder and walk out the door. But we will all experience the death of a relationship or a human that matters to us. All of us need trusted friends and ritual scripts in such moments, though we don't always get them.

The Origin of Ritual Scripts

Scripts proliferate for almost everything we do. The more important moments tend to have more detailed instructions. We script

1. John Steinbeck, *East of Eden* (New York: Penguin Books, 2003), 295.

out weddings and funerals down to the minute. We set the stage, and the recently married or departed play their roles accordingly. I remind myself that all rituals *come from somewhere*. Why do I wash my hands before every meal? Because someone prescribed that cleanliness ritual to me, underscoring the importance of eliminating germs. I believed it, and I embody it with little direct evidence of its actual hygienic powers. It turns out that it can be healthy to wash our hands, but too much germophobia creates health problems, too. Still, if there is a valid hand-washing script to follow, who was its original author? It certainly wasn't my mom.

When we consider all the rituals in our lives, three sources seem to repeatedly emerge as the authors behind most of them:

- God
- our traditions
- the real world

To offer a quick key: Communion is commanded by Jesus as a new covenant rite (i.e., God); classroom rituals are handed down from the experienced to the novice teachers (i.e., traditions); and safety rituals among electricians emerge naturally from their working around lethal voltages and actively trying not to get killed (i.e., the real world).

It's not a matter of whether we'll embody rituals prescribed by others—we are all currently practicing rites rooted in one or more of these three authorities. At some point, we all have to ask: Whose ritual scripts are we following, and why?

Scripts from God: Sacrificing the Red Heifer and Sleeping in Tents[2]

Say that you've just killed a man in combat or found a loved one dead. Now what? If you've lost a person dear to you or committed profound violence, the scriptlessness that follows the question erupts without asking.

The Hebrews were given the "now what" for these situations. Deep within the Torah of Moses, the red heifer sacrifice tells them what to do after they've touched a human corpse (Num. 19:11) or killed someone in battle (Num. 19:16).

The ritual seems a bit weird, even by Old Testament standards. After contact with a dead human, a Hebrew becomes ritually unclean. However, she can be made clean again through the burning of a red heifer outside the camp of Israel and the dispensing of the cow's ashes according to the script.

Not surprisingly, this one ritual has confounded more biblical interpreters than any other. If it merely acts out a symbolic reality, then why a *red* heifer? Why is it killed outside the camp? Why does touching the ashes of the animal make the sacrificer unclean? What is the sacrificer being *purified from* by performing this ritual?

Some scholars think that the ritual purifies Israelites from "death contamination." Maybe it transfers death contamination away from the person and onto the red cow. But focusing too much on an explanation might neglect another key aspect of the ritual: how it shapes the person who has just intimately experienced killing or the death of a loved one.[3]

If we consider that the ritual might teach this person something, other possibilities emerge. Even if the ritual intends to pu-

2. Portions of this section have been adapted from my book *Knowledge by Ritual* (Winona Lake, IN: Eisenbrauns, 2016), 179–80.
3. I am deeply indebted to Joshua Weinstein for his insights and supposals on this ritual.

rify the Israelite from the stain of death, the death-stained participant also needs to know that she is purified.

In other words, dispensing trite sayings—"It's all part of God's plan"—to those struggling with death or the act of killing might not deal effectively with the existential morass caused by their experience. But a ritual gives them a tangible way to begin the long walk out of the inscrutable pangs and confusion of a death so near to them.

Joan Didion, author of *The Year of Magical Thinking*, describes the deepening pain after her husband's death as "the unending absence that follows, the void, the very opposite of meaning, the relentless succession of moments during which we will confront the experience of meaninglessness itself."[4] Those of us who have known the loss of close ones or the fog of combat often don't know what questions to ask, much less how to act. We, like Steinbeck's protagonist, stab in vain at the sea of unanswerable questions.

But our bodies certainly know how to respond, even if our hearts and minds don't. Our understanding of the physiological effects of depression, post-traumatic stress, and more has grown significantly in the last generation. And this brings us back to the red heifer ritual. I can't claim to illumine the mystery surrounding it, but I know this much: the ritual engages the whole person in her body, not merely her mourning soul. It shows her an unambiguous path where the living body and the dead body physically and symbolically diverge from one another. Death must go into the ashes. The living must return to the camp.

A Harvard study on grieving gives us insight into public displays of grief. It points out that the typical American death rituals

---

4. Quoted in Emily Esfahani Smith, "In Grief, Try Personal Rituals: The psychology of rituals in overcoming loss, restoring broken order," *Atlantic* (online), March 14, 2014 (accessed July 16, 2015: http://www.theatlantic.com/health/archive/2014/03/in-grief-try-personal-rituals/284397/). It's interesting to note that Didion wrote this book and then promoted it with numerous readings, thus creating her own ritual of grieving.

actually don't greatly help the grieving. Funeral services, regional mourning practices, obituaries, and the like have less impact than private and personal rituals. Public rituals don't work as well specifically because public grief doesn't offer those grieving any sense of control. What does help? Researchers found that asking participants to perform "a ritual that consisted of a series of behaviors after learning that people often engage in rituals after experiencing a loss was effective."[5]

Indeed, the red heifer sacrifice might teach the Israelite the meaning behind sayings such as "It's all in God's hands" in a way unavailable through any intellectual or emotional exercises. (This is not to diminish or separate intellect from emotions.) As it turns out, researchers found that scripted rituals give mourners a sense of control after the chaos unleashed by death:

> Rituals, which are deliberately controlled gestures, trigger a very specific feeling in mourners—the feeling of being in control of their lives. After people did a ritual or wrote about doing one, they were more likely to report thinking that "things were in check" and less likely to feel "helpless," "powerless," and "out of control."[6]

If death causes us to lose track of the trail, death rituals ought to reorient us and give us a processed path back into the realm of God's charge. We want to return to where things are "in check," even if not under our control. In the bizarre red-cow ritual, scriptlessness meets loving script.

But don't miss the fact that modern scripted death rituals similar to the red heifer ritual work precisely because they give structure to mourning. So it shouldn't surprise us when we find

5. Michael I. Norton and Francesca Gino, "Rituals Alleviate Grieving for Loved Ones, Lovers, and Lotteries," *Journal of Experimental Psychology* 143, no. 1 (2014): 266–72.

6. Smith, "In Grief, Try Personal Rituals."

"deliberately controlled gestures" in the scripted biblical rituals. After all, God gives the Hebrews a wealth of rituals aimed at helping them interpret their grief, their bounty, their sinfulness, and their relationship to God.

All of this raises the important question of authority. By what right does God offer a script for my gestures or my bodily life? In Scripture, God's authority to prescribe stems from being the loving creator of all things.

God scripted ritual instructions for the first couple: "You shall surely eat from all the trees of the garden." And he added a caveat: "But do not eat of the tree of knowledge of good and evil, for in the day that you eat of it, you shall surely die" (Gen. 2:16). What went wrong?

East of Eden—in the Genesis story, not the Steinbeck novel— we imagine that the man and woman had time to reflect on what went wrong in the garden. When they replayed the debacle in their heads, the words of God's indictment must have rung loudly in the man's ears: "Because you listened! Because you listened!"

This seminal story about wrongful listening inaugurates a Scripture-long theme of listening to the right (and wrong) voices. In the infamous story of Eden, Genesis pays close attention to the serpent's wiliness and the couple's eating of the fruit. But the storyline itself homes in on an oft-neglected plot line: To whose voice should they listen?

When the man and woman first hide from God in shame, notice God's first questions. God does not ask the man "How did you figure this all out?" or "How did you deduce this profound truth from the available facts?" God's only questions to the man are "Who told you?," and then "Have you eaten?"

Both questions presume that another voice has entered Eden (Gen. 3:11). God confirms this in the only indictment of wrongdoing in the entire story—"Because you listened to the voice of your wife and ate"—though it's worth noting that the narrator presumes that his wife was also listening to the voice of the serpent (Gen. 3:17).

The Eden story as a whole focuses on listening to the correct voice. This emphasis, found throughout Scripture, means that we will embody the rituals of the people to whom we listen. God scripted a ritual of eating "from every tree in the garden" with one exception (Gen. 2:16–17). Surprisingly, God admonishes the man alone for eating from the prohibited tree of knowledge of good and evil (Gen. 3:17).

What was the man's crime? It was this: Listening to a voice other than God's. Another voice entered the garden, and the man should have known that only his Creator had the right to script rituals of life, death, and wisdom.

Like an infomercial that sells you a product as a gateway "to the life you never knew," the serpent scripted rituals in which the fruit was a portal into another world hoarded away from the man and woman by God. In the end, the serpent didn't lie. Adam and Eve did not die when they ate the forbidden fruit, though death entered their world. Their eyes were opened (Gen. 3:7). And they did indeed become like God, knowing good and evil (Gen. 3:22). In a knotty twist of irony, listening to the serpent gave them the life they never knew—in spades.

This begins a history-long storyline about our ritualed world, and who scripts our rituals and by what authority. It also begins the story of humanity with a view of rituals that we rarely consider today: We perform rituals in community for the sake of knowing.

Further into the Torah, God orchestrates Israel's holy days with rituals for the sake of knowing. Sukkot (also called "the Feast of Booths") requires Israelites to build and live in shelters outside their homes, "that your generations may know that I made the people of Israel dwell in booths when I brought them out of the land of Egypt" (Lev. 23:43). But if the parents want their children to know that they lived in shelters on the way through the wilderness, couldn't they just tell them the facts?

Parents: "Hey kids, just so you know, we lived in tents on our way out of Egypt."

Kids: "Oh, OK."

Not according to God's ritual scripts. Something about the fact that God made them live in shelters needs to be known, and the only way to discern this something is to practice Sukkot every year. Likewise, Passover is to be celebrated annually, specifically so that the generations will know God's mighty acts on behalf of the Hebrews (Exod. 12:26–27).

And so it's no surprise that on an evening of the Passover celebrations in Jerusalem well over a thousand years later, Jesus of Nazareth strategically modifies Passover. He takes a ritual dedicated to correctly remembering God's historic actions in Egypt and inaugurates a new version of that ritual: the Lord's Supper. He ritualizes the ritual. Bold move.

Like the Feast of Booths, Passover, and many of Israel's other rituals, the Lord's Supper is focused on knowing and remembering. Jesus instructs his disciples to practice the Lord's Supper in order to correctly understand God's actions on that night in Jerusalem. Comprehension doesn't come from mere mental reflection, although that is also an embodied ritual activity. To know what Jesus wants to show them, the disciples perform the ritual he scripts for them as a community.

What does this all have to do with authority to give ritual instructions? Scripture affirms throughout that we will know the world according to the voices to whom we listen—for good or for ill. The biblical authors point us back again and again to the God who created every thing and bound himself to Abraham, Isaac, Jacob, and Israel as the primary prescriber of rites. All human rites begin in creation and come to their fullness in the new heavens and earth.

At the beginning of the history of the universe, we find the Creator of everything, who sets humanity in motion with food rituals ("You shall surely eat from all the trees"). Even when they rebel, God redeems his people from Egypt and again gives them scripted food rituals for understanding themselves and their relationship to the world (Passover, manna in the wilderness, sacrificial meals, Sukkot). And when God sends his Son into the world, Jesus, like his Father, leaves his community with a scripted food ritual—the Lord's Supper—in order that they might understand the nature of the kingdom he brings.

Of course, Judaism and Christianity have their own rituals riding on top of the biblical rituals. It's worth considering that rituals like prayer services and funerals are distinct from biblically commanded rituals, like offerings and baptism. Many rituals may be intertwined with biblically commanded rites in churches today. But practitioners beware—the sources of the scripts may vary.

Scripts from Traditions:
Talking to the Dead . . . in a Phone Booth

In his book *The Liturgy of Death*, the Eastern Orthodox theologian Alexander Schmemann attacks the American "funeral machine." Why? The funeral machinery wants to medicalize and conceal death from us, "to render that loss for us, the survivors, into something as painless, smooth, and unnoticeable as possible."[7] Schmemman continues, "In its attitude toward death a culture defines and reveals its understanding . . . of life's meaning and goal."[8]

In other words, American culture creates this script, shaping not only our view of grief but also our view of life itself. Schmemann asks us to consider this question: By what right do we let the "funeral machine" script our death rituals? To broaden the question, we might ask, By what right do we let the machinery of our culture script our daily rituals?

---

7. Alexander Schmemann, *The Liturgy of Death* (Yonkers, NY: St. Vladimir's Seminary Press, 2016), 31.

8. Schmemann, *The Liturgy of Death*, 36.

And what other cultural traditions do we dutifully follow? Who would have thought that survivors could sort out death by a disconnected phone in a booth? After the 2011 tsunami that struck Japan, entire villages mourned the loss of friends and family. How could the communities deal with such pain? When the Japanese "funeral machine" went silent, one man had a simple idea to help people engage with their loss. He transformed a common action—making a phone call—into a grieving ritual: talking to the dead in a phone booth.[9]

This phone booth is normal in every way, except that the phone doesn't "work," at least not in the usual sense of the word. The booth sits secluded on the man's rural property. Though the phone isn't hooked up, the grieving come to connect. Survivors can be seen dialing numbers known only to them, and then they talk to their dead.

The ordinariness of this ritual seems to help them navigate this extraordinary circumstance—it gives them "deliberately controlled gestures" to follow. The conversations they have with their dead sisters, brothers, fathers, mothers, children, friends, and more shock those who haven't spent much time around such grieving. Here's one such conversation from a man to his parents, his wife (Mine), and his infant son (Issei). They all perished in the tsunami. The man speaks these words through the phone in the booth and through his tears.

His pain deserves to be read slowly:

Dad?
Mom?
Mine?
Issei?
It's already been five years since the disaster.

9. http://www.japantimes.co.jp/culture/2016/03/04/tv/phone-booth -contacting-dead-renewal-tsunami-cm-week-brother/#.WPwEflPytE4; https:// www.washingtonpost.com/news/worldviews/wp/2016/03/11/five-years-after -devastating-tsunami-japan-pauses-to-remember/?utm_term=.6c3a55b0261b.

If this voice reaches you, please listen.
Sometimes I don't know what I'm living for.
Issei, Issei, please let me hear you call me Papa.
Even though I built a new house—
Dad? Mom?
Mine and Issei
—without all of you, it's meaningless.
I want to hear your reply, but I can't hear anything.
I'm sorry.
I'm so sorry I couldn't save you.[10]

It's wrenching. How would we console him? What path would we trace out for him to walk? This man is like many others who come here. In this booth, they talk without shame to the dead, as if they were on the other end of the line. The phone in the booth provides familiarity and privacy, and the conversations are strange and soul-bearing at the same time. They expose the farthest reaches of a human's being. The disconnected phone actually works.

In such times, grieving people have to do *something*. So even when a man creates an unusual new tradition, people try it. What's interesting—and significant—is that the mourners' phone booth strategically modifies an everyday practice so that grieving families might be able to discern a way forward—to detect the trail from the sheer jungle of their loss.

Traditions can also create more detailed ritual scripts. Jewish tradition has well-known death rituals for survivors, too. Their rites have historical and faintly biblical roots. For instance, someone must sit with the body of the deceased at all times until burial. Maybe you've heard of it. It's called "sitting *shivah*," *shivah* referring to the seven days of mourning, which include fasting from the normal pleasures of the living.

10. Transcript: https://www.thisamericanlife.org/radio-archives/episode/597/transcript.

After burial, ritual mourning continues. Loved ones may wear torn clothing as a sign of their grief. Different traditions within Judaism may extend the period of mourning to a year, depending on one's relation to the dead. But mourning has final punctuation. After the period of mourning ends, it's no longer appropriate to mourn.

For most Jews, these rituals are not optional. The community expects them, just as Christians usually expect a memorial service and a cemetery burial. Despite the cultural pressure to perform these rituals, that pressure doesn't necessarily diminish their value to mourners.

Though not particularly religious anymore, Jonathan Safran Foer writes about this aspect of Jewish death rituals, noting that we need such "deliberately controlled gestures":

> Judaism gets death right. It instructs us what to do when we know least well what to do and feel an overwhelming need to do something. You should sit like this. We will. You should dress like this. We will. You should say these words at these moments, even if you have to read from transliteration. I think that really captures very well how ritual can be very helpful at times when you don't know what to do or what to say or how to dress. And, you know, the Jewish rituals for mourning the dead tell you what to do for all those things.[11]

Traditions offer numerous helpful rites, and that may also make some of us nervous. The problem with traditions authoring our rituals may feel like a long train coming. As my religious Jewish friends tell me, they've been struggling with this problem for millennia. They feel the weight of their wealth of ritual traditions, and this forces the big question: Where do my daily and regular rituals find their roots, and according to whom?

---

11. Jonathan Safran Foer, *Here I Am* (New York: Farrar, Straus and Giroux, 2016), 370.

On the whole, religious Jews tend to think of their religion not in terms of theology, but in terms of practice. What do we do when we're in situation X, Y, or Z? Should my ritual scripts come from deep within the history of my tradition, or can I improvise? The resolution to such quandaries always mixes tradition and improvisation, but should the ratio lean more toward past traditions or toward present freedom to improvise? In other words, who makes this stuff up?

Christians face a similar quandary today. Although Christian tradition is centuries-long and rich in ritual, many of us have to plead ignorant of its existence, much less its bounty. In the book *Deep Church Rising*, the authors suggest that we delve deep into the historic and "small-c" catholic rituals of the church. By studying and re-appropriating the ritualed life that the church has always prized, we can find a safe way forward:

> We cannot be living (in) deep church if we know little or nothing about what the church has learned from experience, where and when it (or members of it) took a wrong turn, what victories it achieved, and how it learned to articulate the truths of revelation.[12]

Maybe you, like so many of us, shiver at the thought of studying Scripture and the history of the church in order to be guided by them today. But the sober reality is that you are currently being guided by many religious and cultural rituals already scripted out for you.

The "funeral machine" has already scripted your final service, just as the "wedding machine" has already planned your nuptial day. The "worship music machine" has already ritualized your Sunday morning songs. The "sports machine" has scripted and

---

12. Andrew G. Walker and Robin A. Parry, *Deep Church Rising: The Third Schism and the Recovery of Orthodoxy* (Eugene, OR: Cascade, 2014), 14.

ritualized your leisure time. The "fitness machine" has scripted your exercise, which then shapes your vision of what an acceptable body looks like and maybe the shame or hubris that accompanies it.

The "fashion machine" has scripted every color, fabric, and cut that you are ritually wearing. The "successful career machine," "career-family balance machine," and more are pumping out the scripts of your rituals like priestly monkeys banging on liturgical typewriters. Need I go on?

And all good rituals can be twisted, perverted toward an end not intended by God. Family meals can be gluttonized. Nutrition can be anorexized. Exercise can descend into egoistic sports competitions and body bragging. Parenting can devolve into power struggles. Sexual intimacy can contort into pornographic re-enactments. Scripture reading can be corrupted into daily doses of bibliolatry, a worship of the Bible itself. As one witty person quipped to me, "It's a ritual-eat-ritual world."[13]

The cultural monkeys continually write and publish scripts for us, voices to whom we already listen. Yet Scripture reiterates throughout that we must understand God's instruction *and how it has gone wrong.* Only then can we faithfully improvise our ritualed lives in community.

Scripts from the World around Us:
Deep Lessons from the Cosmos

"There is surely no more useful skill in the practice of scientific research than the knack for not accidentally killing oneself with the laboratory equipment."[14] This is the first sentence of a study

---

13. Thanks to Taylor Lindsay for giving me that phrase!

14. Benjamin Sims, "Safe Science: Material and Social Order in Laboratory Work," *Social Studies of Science* 35, no. 3 (June 2005): 333.

by Benjamin Sims on scientists who work with high-powered lasers at Los Alamos National Laboratory in New Mexico. It wins the award for "best first sentence of a science article ever." This government lab hosts dangerous work, and mistakes can maim or kill researchers. For this reason, these scientists have built up an arsenal of rituals that protect them, but also teach concepts vital for life.

Remarkably, when looking for groups comparable to these laser researchers, Sims found that their behaviors were most like those of the biblical priests who worked around the dangerous presence of God in the Tabernacle. Researchers at Los Alamos have developed cleanliness rites like those found in Leviticus, rites for caring about others, and all kinds of rituals for making sure no one gets hurt while the work continues successfully.

That rituals will inevitably emerge from our routines is a fact that doesn't need proving. We'll dry off in the shower the same way every day out of habit—no attention necessary. If we've almost crashed into a car on the way to work because we didn't check our blind spots before a lane change, we'll start systematically checking our mirrors before switching lanes.

Reality crashes into our ritualed world and yields, well, new rituals. Anytime we do something repeatedly or figure out how dangerous a piece of equipment can be, we script rituals—like those scientists did—to make it more efficient or safe.

A big-picture concern confronts us now. If the God of Israel and Christianity created the cosmos and orchestrates it today, then to ignore created reality as a source of ritual instruction means that we might be ignoring the Creator. In fact, Israel's understanding of God demands learning from creation itself.

Prophets regularly thumped Israel because they ignored the fact that God withheld the rains from them for a reason (Jer. 3:3; Hag. 1:10; Amos 4:7). God intended the lack of rain to re-orient their sacrifices away from foreign gods and back to the God of Israel. Yet, even when God did send the rains and the land produced abundantly, Israel often sacrificed their produce in thanks to Ba'al, the Canaanite god of rain (Hos. 2:8). Then the created cosmos objectively confronted Israel with God's judgment of their rituals.

Yes, reality shapes our behaviors. But there's more: paying sober attention to the real world yields the skills needed to interpret God's revelation to us. In the book of Luke, Jesus lambastes the gathered crowds because they have allowed reality to script their agricultural rites, when to sow and when to harvest. Yet they don't use the same skills "to interpret the present time" (Luke 12:56). Why does Jesus chastise them? Because they observe the winds and clouds in order to guide their care for the wheat growing in the field. But they don't allow the reality of Jesus's signs and wonders to guide their response to God. So he calls them hypocrites.

From our successes and failures in interacting with the real world, ritual practices emerge. It's inevitable. The Christian Scriptures emphasize reality's reach into us as humans in a way that is genuinely unique to Judeo-Christianity: this created world is real and has the right to teach us, and therefore shape our embodied practices. As Jesus reminds us, the rituals fostered from our repeated encounters with creation help us understand the invisible kingdom of God. Failing to soberly engage the created world might ultimately foster a deaf ear toward the Creator himself.

Who's Making up Our Rituals?

If we're believers, and if we're paying close attention, we know that God has constructed a base camp of rituals for us, but also guidance for all the rest of our ritualed life. In fact, God seems to have structured humanity's existence in rituals. Directed by the prophets, we improvise with what's been handed down through traditions.

Of course, we aren't the only ones with good ritual practices— think of the phone booth to the dead in Japan. But God does hold us specifically accountable, like the man in Eden, for the voices to whom we listen. If the Eden account tells us anything, it warns us about whose voice ought to script our rituals and to what end.

What I'd like to suggest is that we find safer harbors together, going deep into the rituals in Scripture shaped by the history of faithful ritual improvisation. The church won't have gotten rites right all the time, but it will offer us guidance on essential practices and ways to improvise without violating the scripts of Scripture. Which means no more priestly monkeys banging on ritual typewriters.

Chapter 4

All Journeys Have a Secret Destination

However much man may toil in seeking,
he will not find it out.
Even though a wise man claims to know,
he cannot find it out.

Ecclesiastes 8:16–17

The end of the matter; all has been heard.
Fear God and keep his commandments,
for this is the whole duty of man.
For God will bring every deed into judgment,
with every secret thing, whether good or evil.

Ecclesiastes 12:13–14

I sometimes give odd assignments to my students. In studies of the Psalms, I've had students write limericks that summarized Israel's exodus from Egypt or the creation story. The first time I assigned this task, students complained. They couldn't understand how writing a campy English poem (yes, the oldest limericks hail from England) had anything to do with a biblical literature course.

Trust doesn't come easy, especially if we can't see the connection between what someone is asking us to do and how it will cause us to know something. The Jewish philosopher Martin Buber shrewdly claimed, "All journeys have a secret destination of which the traveler is unaware." We can't always see the connections between our efforts and the outcomes they garner. But if we need someone to guide us, then we won't always be able to understand the reasons behind the rituals of learning they prescribe. My case in point: constructing a limerick offers many advantages to understanding ancient Hebrew poetry, but only if students trust the professor and do the assignment as instructed.

"However much man may toil in seeking, he will not find it out." The unsettling certainty of the author of Ecclesiastes ought to disturb us. Early on in the book, the author claims that he has the reason, the resources, and the experience to figure out the basic mechanisms of the world around us. Yet, after an exhaustive search, he can't do it. And he claims that if a wise man says that he has everything figured out, then he is deceived. Is this the big "Oh, well" moment in Hebrew Scripture—giving up any hope of understanding the world? If so, then what do we do now?

According to Ecclesiastes, we should practice the instruction of the Torah (the rituals in the books of Moses) in reverence to a God who can judge us. The injunction to "keep his commandments" includes practicing all the rituals of purity, sacrifice, and the festivals. Jesus practiced all of these, and so did his disciples. In the end, Ecclesiastes points to God as the one who should script our rites—after all, he knows "every secret thing."

Is Ecclesiastes suggesting that we ought to practice the rituals blindly? Does wisdom require that we understand *that we cannot understand*?

At no point in my life have I figured it all out. But I do remember feeling as if I could at various times. And so have others. No shortage of intellectuals and charismatic "thought leaders" have claimed to have mastered mathematics, physics, politics, or human behavior, only to find out that they overestimated their own abilities or underestimated the rich complexity of the world, or both.

I've muddled through cycles of wanting to understand it all, even if in some small sphere of life: biblical history, jazz drumming, psychological motivations of the skinhead movement, and more. After hitting some impenetrable wall of ignorance, I gave up the quest for total certainty. I was trying to conquer an area of knowledge rather than participate in a discerning community. It never worked.

But maybe we don't need to understand how rituals work *on* us in order for them to work *in* us. Insisting on figuring out how rituals foster understanding might even be destructive to the very things that rituals do best: teach us to see what was always there right in front of us. In biblical language, rituals teach us to *see truly*—to grasp reality in high definition.

After practicing the ritual of fasting, we can embody it comfortably. Only then might we see through it to what it shows us about ourselves and our relationships to others. Only then can we look back at it and understand how the parts contribute to the whole. Only then can we begin thinking about how the ritual of fasting works.

So, here's the (admittedly) controversial claim: You don't need to know what the bread and wine of the Lord's Supper *are* in order for Communion to do what it's meant to *do*. Not only is that OK—it's necessary. The same goes for the waters of baptism, the words of pronouncement at a wedding, essay assignments in college classes, the fist my mechanic made to illustrate a cracked piston, and so on.

Understanding comes by rituals of learning, but only when we look back on the whole process after we've had a *eureka!* moment. My Air Force training makes the case. Only after I clearly understood an aspect of radar theory could I then point back to the rites that allowed me to grasp those abstract radio-frequency principles. How could I know that the rituals would guide me to such epiphanies while I was performing them? I couldn't. I had to trust my instructors and embody their directions in order to see what they were showing me. Once I grasped the principles, I could sometimes identify how they worked; only then could I offer scripted rites to others.

An Example: Ritualizing Trauma

How can talking about our feelings harm some people? The psychiatrist Bessel van der Kolk discusses the first time he realized that traumatized Vietnam veterans weren't getting better by talking about their feelings or experiences.[1] In fact, the ritual of group therapy discussions often re-traumatized his patients. At some point Van der Kolk recognized that his psychiatric training had given him a shoddy model of the human person. Poor models of humans make for impoverished rituals. The evidence of the model's defectiveness sat in chairs arranged in a circle at the VA hospital week after week.

The therapies he had been trained to perform actually made his patients worse. Eventually, a new diagnosis called Post-Traumatic Stress Disorder (PTSD) would account for what he saw in those years after the Vietnam War. Van der Kolk was learning what many of us wouldn't find out until later: that a decade after the war had ceased in Vietnam, the battles still raged on in the *bodies* of these veterans.

What was the problem with the old model of human psychology? It presumed that there was a soul inside the person and that

1. This section is gleaned from Bessel van der Kolk's *The Body Keeps the Score: Brain, Mind, and Body in the Healing of Trauma* (New York: Penguin Books, 2014).

emotional traumas hurt the non-physical part of the person. These veterans wrestled with the pangs of violating moral standards—watching friends being maimed or die, realizing that people had tried to kill them, coming to grips with their own attempts to kill those people, and so on. Because of the thinking of the time, Dr. van der Kolk applied emotional therapies to emotional problems, just as his training had taught him.

But his veterans experienced flashbacks, full-body reactions to harmless triggers. Sometimes they had flashbacks just from talking about their traumatic experiences. Who would have thought that talking it out might actually do more harm than good? After a few years, van der Kolk realized that treatment for PTSD had to include the body as well as the mind.

When triggered by the explosion of fireworks, certain smells, certain memories, and more, the bodies of these men reacted as if they were back in battle. Their adrenal systems pumped full-bore. Their fight-or-flight mentality took over their behaviors. And even after these episodes subsided, their bodies' reactions to the unreal trauma didn't go away.

No matter how safe they knew they were, intellectually speaking, their built-in protection systems possessed them completely. And van der Kolk now understood something that made matters worse: that these vets were stuck in their past traumas, unable to figure out that no danger was actually present now.

Over the decades, many therapies were developed to treat PTSD. (PTSD is not only a veterans' issue; numbers indicate that it affects more rape victims and children of abuse than combat veterans.) These therapies included common-sense rituals such as journaling, joining support groups, taking medication, participating in community theatre, and others that you could probably guess.

But the problem had to be addressed more directly. So van der Kolk began to use a new therapy that engaged the veterans' bodies. Discovered almost by accident, one treatment relied on an odd form of distraction called Eye Movement Desensitization and Reprocessing (EMDR) therapy.

In EMDR therapy, the patient visually tracked van der Kolk's fingers as he moved them back and forth, left to right, in front of the patient. As the patient's eyes moved, the doctor guided him to reflect on past traumas and allow his mind to pull up triggering memories, images, smells, and so on. His fingers continued to move tick-tock, like a metronome, so the patient's eyes moved rapidly back and forth.

This bizarre therapy allowed patients to revisit their trauma without its associated reactions in their adrenal systems. It allowed them to process what happened and its effect on their present life, which enabled some of them to detach from their traumas. It turned out that traumatized patients who trusted a doctor enough to perform this strange therapy got better sometimes, even if they didn't understand how the ritual worked.

EMDR therapy strategically ritualizes the remembrance of past events so that patients can successfully process trauma. It trains the whole body to perceive the present situation correctly so that it's not wrongly triggered into combat mode. After all, we need adrenaline and hypersensitivity only in dangerous situations, not while sitting in our living room with our family. As van der Kolk says, "For real change to take place, *the body needs to learn* that the danger has passed and to live in the reality of the present."[2]

Trust: The Ritual Glue

In their best uses, rituals teach us how to see more truly, and for us to do that, our bodies must be involved. If a ritual is going to work, we can't attempt to figure it out while participating in it. This seems to denigrate the very purpose of the ritual.

2. Van der Kolk, *The Body Keeps the Score*, 21; italics mine.

Until we see what the ritual tries to show us, ritual scripts will always puzzle us.

So how does a doctor get a patient to participate in the odd ritual of EMDR? Researchers don't even know how it works. It comes back to the issue of trust. Obviously, a patient needs to trust the doctor's training and accreditation. But if she's being plagued by a life-altering trauma, wouldn't this seem a little kooky? What would compel her to do it? If she knew that it worked for others, would that make her trust the ritual script, even if she didn't understand it?

This exact problem of ritual puzzlement shows up in the Hebrew Bible. When the prophet Elisha tells the leprous Naaman to baptize himself in the Jordan River, Naaman openly puzzles at the command: "I thought that . . . he would wave his hand over the spot and cure the leprosy" (2 Kings 5:11). Elisha insists on his dipping himself seven times in the Jordan River, a specific and involved ritual that Naaman cannot understand.

Nothing but trust in Elisha, who had reportedly healed many people and raised the dead, would allow Naaman to glimpse a leprosy-free life and something about the God who could heal him. The story ends not just with Naaman's healing from leprosy, but with his declaring what he now knows because of the ritual: "Now I know that there is no God in all the earth except in Israel" (2 Kings 5:15).

This might remind us of the placebo effect. Provided that the doctor seems concerned and confident and provides a diagnosis, placebos work even when the patient knows that she's being given sugar pills. Trust is what makes the placebos effective.[3] For placebos to work, the normal practice of eating becomes ritualized into pill consumption. It becomes like a sacrament that shapes the

3. Ted J. Kaptchuk, "The Placebo Effect in Alternative Medicine: Can the Performance of a Healing Ritual Have Clinical Significance?" *Annals of Internal Medicine* 136, no. 11 (June 2002): 817–25.

entire being of the person, revealing her trust in the caring ritual-prescriber. It's not hard to see how this corresponds to God's design of humans as ritualed creatures, especially considering God's use of food rituals throughout the Scriptures.

God's rituals given in the creation and the life prescribed in the Torah continue to be fruitful throughout the ages and into the New Testament. In the Gospels, Jesus doesn't invent new rituals, but strategically changes the rituals from the Torah. All of these rituals work only if we trust God as a caring ritual-prescriber.

Whether a ritual works doesn't depend on our being able to understand its actions or decode them in advance. With ritual, as with all learning, we put our trust in those who rightly teach us.

Doing the Right Thing: Not Figuring Rites Out

So why does Ecclesiastes tell us to give up figuring it all out? According to the Eden story in Genesis, humans were created not to figure everything out in advance, but to trust the voice of God. God is depicted as taking care when he created this world and placed us in it. Humanity made its first mistake by trying to understand the world apart from God's guidance, and under the guidance of a dubious voice.

We've already talked about Passover as a ritual of learning for Hebrew children. The puzzling rite prompted them to ask for explanations, so parents were commissioned to teach them how the odd bits of the meal connected to their history and to God: "By a strong hand Yahweh brought us out of Egypt, from the house of slavery" (Exod. 13:14). With this momentous change, the Hebrews became God's servants (Lev. 25:55). Thus the Passover night of freedom became an annual classroom for Hebrew children. Moses instructed the parents, "And when in time to come your son asks you, 'What is this [ritual]?' You shall say to him . . ." (Exod. 13:14).

Joshua followed suit with his pile of stones on the side of the Jordan River. "When your sons ask their fathers in times to come, 'What do these stones mean to you all?'" (Josh. 4:21), the twelve stones represent the answer. They stand for the time when God dried up the waters of the Jordan so that the Israelites could cross over safely. They teach us of God's might to his people and "all the peoples of the earth." They represent part of the way Israel is meant to act and, therefore, think about the world.

Going against the grain of how we think about facts and knowledge, the Torah teaches that we are forever separated from that which we need to know—life-and-death matters of knowledge—if we don't perform the rituals prescribed by God. Rites always have an invisible arrow through them, pointing toward something else. They dispose us to see something being shown to us, both past and present. Wisdom and understanding come from sitting at the feet of wise instructors.

The coaches in our lives will inevitably give us puzzling instructions we must embody in order to understand. Eating bread and drinking wine as if it's flesh and blood doesn't have immediate or obvious benefits, but performing this ritual over time does. As the author Wesley Hill once said about his spells of depression and the ritual of going to weekly church, "In my experience, going to church on a given Sunday doesn't often help. But going to church for many Sundays during a dark year does."

Although these practices don't convey information to us, biblical authors insist from beginning to end that rituals do indeed teach us. And this isn't only true for religious understanding. Because our world has been structured to teach through ritual, and knowing is not a mere transfer of data, the instructions for knowing will often perplex us.

Until Hollywood showed us, we couldn't conceive of how ordinary physical tasks could shape karate skills in a young man's body. In the film *The Karate Kid*, a teenage Daniel LaRusso wants to learn karate so that he can fight the boy at high school who's bullying him. After figuring out that the maintenance man at his apartment complex—Mr. Miyagi—is a martial arts master, Daniel seeks to train under him.

When Mr. Miyagi agrees to coach him, they begin with a pact that essentially requires Daniel to perform whatever actions Mr. Miyagi prescribes, *no questions asked*. Mr. Miyagi assumes in his pact that the directions will puzzle Daniel.

> Miyagi: I promise teach karate. That's my part. You promise learn. I say, you do, no questions. That's your part. Deal?
> Daniel: It's a deal.
> Miyagi: First wash all the cars, then wax.
> Daniel: Why do I have to . . .
> Miyagi: Remember deal. No questions.
> Daniel: Yeah, but . . .
> Miyagi: Wax on, right hand. Wax off, left hand.

Daniel, now called Daniel-*san*, presumes that Mr. Miyagi will hand over the secrets to the kingdom of karate. But Mr. Miyagi has other plans, better plans. He wants Daniel-*san*'s entire body to know the world differently. To this end, Daniel-*san*'s karate training consists of washing and waxing cars, painting fences and a house, and sanding a deck.

To train him, Mr. Miyagi ritualizes ordinary practices so that Daniel-*san*'s whole being will understand karate. After days of hard labor, Daniel-*san* suspects that this is all a ruse by Mr. Miyagi to get free labor out of him. Daniel finally snaps, throwing down the worn-out sandpaper onto the smooth deck in defiance. With the tattered sandpaper on the deck between them, he threatens to quit his so-called training.

In response, Mr. Miyagi demonstrates that he has indeed been training the young Daniel-*san*. He stands face-to-face with Daniel-*san* and attacks him with punches and kicks accompanied by shouts. Daniel-*san* semi-miraculously defends himself with the ritualized moves developed in his body through washing, waxing, painting, and sanding. Initially perplexed by the scripts for his karate training, he now grasps what he was learning the whole time. This is how the martial art becomes part of him. The movie proves that "All journeys have a secret destination of which the traveler is unaware."

We've all been in a situation like Daniel-*san*'s, who stands slack-jawed at his own knowledge of karate secretly imbued in him through simple chores. This powerful scene from an admittedly cheesy film speaks profound truths beyond karate, even into the sciences.

In training to be a surgeon, for example, a medical student will be asked to perform a variety of perplexing rituals. But in order for those rites to work, she can't question professors on every assignment and task they prescribe.

The student trusts her professors for a variety of reasons—the accreditation of the university, its place in the rankings, its word-of-mouth prestige, and so forth. But let's not fool ourselves. Just like karate training, surgical training is a series of puzzling rituals prescribed with a deep sense of "Trust us—we know what we're doing" built in. Like Mr. Miyagi, professors secretly develop skills in a student's whole person. Once again proving that "All journeys have a secret destination of which the traveler is unaware."

As ritualed creatures, we understand that we can't come to know most things apart from practicing the puzzling scripts given to us. Yet somehow, this trust that we extend to doctors and professors dead-ends with our religious communities. We try to figure out how eating bread and drinking wine within a church community does anything at all. Or we assume it doesn't affect anything beyond mere performance. We might as well be banging on the disconnected "Close Door" button in the elevator.

But if sacraments dispose us to understand this world in certain ways—and that's how they're presented in Scripture—they aren't about decoding. Trusting, even when we don't understand how a sacrament works or what its purpose is, affirms the One in whom we trust.

Because I'm not able to make scripts for myself, I've learned to trust those who have earned the right to script the rituals I need. And so I return to the wisdom of Ecclesiastes:

> The end of the matter; all has been heard.
> Fear God and keep his commandments,
> for this is the whole duty of man.
> For God will bring every deed into judgment,
> with every secret thing, whether good or evil.
>
> (Eccles. 12:13–14)

WHEN RITES GO WRONG

Chapter 5

When Rites Go Dark

Train up a child in either Apple or Android;
and even when they are old they will not depart from it.

Jennifer Grassman, "Internet Proverbs"

It's no accident that smoking a cigarette is like reading a short story. It has a setting (getting outside to the smoke hole), a beginning (lighting it up), a middle (calming the nicotine pangs while puffing clouds), a conclusion (snuffing it out), and actions that continue beyond the story (happily ever after—until the pangs start up again). Sucking smoke into our lungs has been eloquently ritualized, narrated, and flavored to perfection. Each smoke break creates a little completed quest.

It's no accident that the smartphone wasn't designed for the human brain. It interrupts and transgresses our focus without a thought about our body's nature. If our phone vibrates in our pocket, our adrenaline kicks up, and we stop in the middle of the sidewalk. Piqued by our desire to be included in something, we dutifully press the virtual "button" on the screen and investigate. As Cat Stevens once crooned, "It's not easy to be calm when you've found something going on," much less when it's found you!

And it's no accident that these twists on rites dig their claws into us in the most unexpected places. Some have criticized the ritualization of nightly TV news-watching, specifically cable news, which features more punditry than journalism. Molly Worthen writes, "The reason Fox News is so formative is that it's this repetitive, almost ritualistic thing that people do every night.... It forms in them particular fears and desires, an idea of America."[1] But surely that critique isn't restricted to Fox News.

Ritualized by devices, media diet, and vices, I do as the script dictates. It's curious that at the same time, I'll catch myself wondering if certain scripts are worth it. Should I go through all the fuss of partaking in the Lord's Supper in church when I'm not sure what it even does for me? My own ritual life is sometimes incoherent to me. Ritual in, ritual out. Ritual in, expected behavior out.

Rites Gone Wrong

We've been tacking on "for good or for ill" to all this rites talk. And now it's time to talk candidly about the "for ill" part of that. Have you heard about the ad agencies steeped in the art of filmmaking, designing commercials to enchant us with their products? Do you know that casinos ooze with rituals aiming to maximize the human ability to sit, stare, and spend money? To help ritualize their facilities, gambling houses rely on the best social-psychology research that academia provides.

And speaking of "for ill" . . . By the time I was twelve years old, I was smoking in earnest. Smokes came easily to children in the 1980s, pre-packaged with a built-in narrative and a ritual. I bought into the ad campaigns which implied that smoking makes you look

---

1. Molly Worthen, "How to Escape from Roy Moore's Evangelicalism," https://www.nytimes.com/2017/11/17/opinion/sunday/escape-roy-moores -evangelicalism.html.

cool. For me, smoking bestowed "street cred." I looked tougher and older—two things I desperately wanted to be. Smoking gave my fidgety body something to do with my hands, my mouth, and my lungs. And like a child seeing his breath on the first icy morning of autumn, I never tired of slowly blowing out clouds of smoke. Cigarette companies knew these things about me, too. By fifteen, I exhibited all the signs of addiction. Smoking up to two packs a day, I continued for eight more years.

One thing became clear to me over that decade of profound addiction: I had ritualized myself into slavery. And I hated it. I know, with more intimacy than I can describe on a page, what the cold shackles of addiction feel like. It turns out that nicotine is one of the most addictive substances studied, more addictive for some than heroin or crack cocaine.

Tapping into a web of humanity's ritual needs, the tobacco industry wrangled those needs into a white paper-wrapped package, tidy and smokable. For even greater ill, they gave a narrative and an identity to smoking through relentless advertising, sometimes aimed directly at children like me.

Addictive Technologies

We've seen the long-term good of ritual (for learning through the body, for increasing understanding). But as all of us know, rituals can also go dark. When motivated by perverse incentives, we can bend good human practices toward corrupt knowledge of ourselves and the world.

In his book *Irresistible: The Rise of Addictive Technology*, Adam Alter charts the frightening waters of technology design.[2] The success of addictive technology runs on its ability to keep us

2. Adam Alter, *Irresistible: The Rise of Addictive Technology* (New York: Penguin, 2017).

hooked—to ritualize its users. When designing a video game or smartphone "app," technology companies actually do so in a way that will conscript our bodies entirely. The monetary success of most of these businesses depends on our "time on screen." For tech companies, it's a ritual-eat-ritual world—*who can get whom to do what for how long with their bodies.*

Alter details how companies have borrowed models from gambling design in order keep us on our devices (like the casino's model to keep players in front of slot machines). Using rewards—providing a sense of mission, offering buzzes and beeps that cue our hormonal system, meeting the felt need for companionship, and more—they've mastered the science of keeping us glued to our screens.

Just as PTSD distorts the limbic system and the neurotransmitters released in the brain, our electronic gadgets home in on getting us to release endorphins and dopamine at just the right times. Their designs keep us on their media, their apps, and their games. They script our day by conscripting our time, our bodies, and our attention with hooks. These hooks range from checking "likes" on social media to next-episode auto-play on TV-viewing sites.

Alter was astonished to discover that the heads of these technology companies often don't allow "smart" devices in their own homes. And many Silicon Valley executives send their kids to schools that ban personal electronics. Steve Jobs famously revealed to a prominent journalist his surprising parental decisions about technology. In his 2014 *New York Times* piece, Nick Bilton recalls his shock at discovering Jobs's stance:

> "So, your kids must love the iPad?" I asked Mr. Jobs, trying to change the subject. The company's first tablet was just hitting the shelves. "They haven't used it," he told me. "We limit how much technology our kids use at home."
>
> I'm sure I responded with a gasp and dumbfounded silence. I had imagined the Jobs's household was like a nerd's paradise: that the walls were giant touch screens, the dining table was

made from tiles of iPads, and that iPods were handed out to guests like chocolates on a pillow.

Nope, Mr. Jobs told me, not even close.

Since then, I've met a number of technology chief executives and venture capitalists who say similar things: they strictly limit their children's screen time, often banning all gadgets on school nights, and allocating ascetic time limits on weekends.

I was perplexed by this parenting style. After all, most parents seem to take the opposite approach, letting their children bathe in the glow of tablets, smartphones and computers, day and night.

Yet these tech C.E.O.'s seem to know something that the rest of us don't.[3]

Even former Google and Facebook executives have admitted their designs lean toward addiction and called for ethics consultants to evaluate child addiction.[4]

Alter's book rewards the reader. Ultimately, he suggests, the antidote to such addictions comes through being more intentional about how we spend our time and seeking natural spaces that are "hook free"—maybe taking a long, phone-free walk where the mind can wander. This is one of the best practices for our mental health, and likely our physical health, too. In fact, recent studies on cognition show that distraction-free walks in green spaces improve our working memory, reduce anxiety, and allow us to think more clearly.[5] Doctors are even beginning to write out prescriptions for "ecotherapy" to their patients.

3. Nick Bilton, "Steve Jobs Was a Low-Tech Parent," https://www.nytimes.com/2014/09/11/fashion/steve-jobs-apple-was-a-low-tech-parent.html.

4. Naomi Schaefer Riley, "America's Real Digital Divide," htttps://www.nytimes.com/2018/02/11/opinion/america-digital-divide.html.

5. For example, Gregory N. Bratman et al., "The Benefits of Nature Experience: Improved Affect and Cognition," *Landscape and Urban Planning* 138 (June 2015): 41–50.

In addition, psychologists now recommend lots of unscripted time for children, time enough for boredom to set in, to give them the chance to develop the ability to structure their thoughts and learn how to prioritize—the so-called *executive* functions.[6] That's right—we prescribe scriptless time, just like our parents did so haphazardly back in the day. In this way we foster the basic skills of becoming functioning adults, what college students now call "adulting." But if kids have constant access to new and stimulating devices, they will lose this precious chance for essential development. Dark rituals indeed.

Twisted Scripts

In an acute irony, we puzzle at the ritual instructions given to us by experts, but unquestioningly embody the ritual scripts handed to us in modern media consumption. We're not puzzled by them—but the aims underlying these rituals may not align with ours. Binge-watching TV shows, for example, heeds a ritual script carefully designed to make us into certain kinds of watchers. And "notifications" on our smartphones interrupt our neurological attention center and ritualize our attention span according to the app designer's goals. And speaking of attention span—that was a long sentence in the digital age. Did you make it all the way through?

We have evidence that smartphones make us demonstrably dumber. Just having them in the same room with us links to lower intellectual ability. Nicholas Carr makes sobering observa-

6. Sherry Turkle is magisterial on this: *Alone Together: Why We Expect More from Technology and Less from Each Other* (New York: Basic Books, 2012). Jean M. Twenge's book title says it all in the most terrifying way possible: *iGen: Why Today's Super-Connected Kids Are Growing Up Less Rebellious, More Tolerant, Less Happy—and Completely Unprepared for Adulthood—and What That Means for the Rest of Us* (New York: Atria Books, 2017).

tions about the cigarette-like relationship we've developed with smartphones:

> So what happens to our minds when we allow a single tool such dominion over our perception and cognition? Scientists have begun exploring that question—and what they're discovering is both fascinating and troubling. Not only do our phones shape our thoughts in deep and complicated ways, but the effects persist even when we aren't using the devices. As the brain grows dependent on the technology, the research suggests, the intellect weakens. . . . Phone makers like Apple and Samsung and app writers like Facebook and Google design their products to consume as much of our attention as possible during every one of our waking hours. . . .[7]

Of course, smartphones and other electronics can bring pleasurable enjoyment. And none of these technologies have injected brand-new problems into a consumer-driven economy. But the delivery systems have changed. And our phones aren't just tools—we've become emotionally attached to them. Most of us carry our phones in our pockets, so they touch our bodies, which causes our brains to wire them into our neurology. What's new: the phone in our pocket now ties into our hormone system. This relationship has changed—it's stronger and faster than what we've ever known before.

How ironic that we refuse to engage when we can't make sense of a healthy ritual script. How many of us would wax the cars and sand the floors of Mr. Miyagi's house in order to know karate?

7. Nicholas Carr, "How Smartphones Hijack Our Minds," *Wall Street Journal,* October 6, 2017, https://www.wsj.com/articles/howsmartphoneshijackour minds1507307811/.

Walk It Off

The ritual of walking borders on the magical. If ill motives have been ritualized into us, then caring acts must ritualize them out of us. This is why I often take students on walks around Lower Manhattan. The crowded sidewalks and the panoply of sights and smells in New York City provide an oddly private space for us to talk.

Sometimes students are wrestling with their first existential crisis or shame at their life choices. Whatever the problem, they're often confused by this phase of their existence. Life has become more complicated than Disney-channel shows led them to believe. Pornography and video games turn more addicting than they could have imagined. Cultural scripts offer easy ruts to fall into. Expectations for American-style success shape their decisions more often than they'd like to admit. In short, they've come to realize that everything around them wants to ritualize them, for good or for ill.

So I take them on walks. Naturally, they want direct answers to the big questions. They want to puzzle it all out and make sense of the cacophony of thoughts and feelings confronting them. So we keep walking. I prod them with questions as the urbane fragrances of New York mark our progress. We dig into their issues near the food carts, move through their insecurities in the salty air near the piers, and come to a point of clarity through the moist sewer steam.

Never, at the end of one of these walks, has anyone said, "Well, now I feel completely better about all that!" But I walk with them regardless. The problems they face can't be resolved by a single missing piece of information, as they had hoped. Whatever knotty situation they currently face, it wasn't sorted into them by a single piece of information; neither will it be sorted out that way.

When they reflect further on their current perplexities, they discover that their problems often stem from years of ritual habits. These habits, sometimes chosen by them and other times chosen for them, deformed their thinking about themselves, the world, God, and so on. Their bodies have been rehearsing these cultural scripts, uncritically acting them out for years. Their parents and others goaded them with both stated and implied expectations, modeled behaviors, and romantic ideals built up by the unceasing barrage of media assaulting them since their childhood.

As we stroll past the coffee shop, surrounded by its brewing aromas, students sometimes see it for themselves. Objective reality eventually crashes in, as is its habit. They haven't become who they thought they'd be. Shining a sobering light on their romantic ideals of success has revealed compromises they didn't want to make. As the sheen of their dreams dulls, everything becomes more complex than they had conceived. Basically, they're coming to terms with that mean old author of Ecclesiastes, who once boldly claimed, "However much man may toil in seeking, he will not find it out."

So we walk, and if I've earned the right to be heard, I might prescribe some rites for them. I offer rituals for seeing their real-life problems with more clarity, not instantaneous cures or fix-alls. And when I prescribe, telling them what they might do, I often see the hope drain from their eyes:

> Go for daily walks, an hour long, and let your mind wander without the help of music.
> Get involved in a small church that acts out biblical forms of justice.
> Read big chunks of Scripture, a book at a time.
> Follow a regular schedule, sleep well, and wake early. Exercise.
> Get rid of your smartphone, or at least severely restrict your usage.
> Don't text people, but talk only face to face or over the phone.
> (I usually have to explain to them that their phones have

an antiquated feature that allows them to call other phones and actually talk by means of their voice with other people.)

They hate me a little when I give them this list, sighing with "Really—that's all you've got?" exasperation. It's as if I asked them to wax my car and sand my deck in order to see their problems more clearly. And that's essentially what I did.

Those who do take these rites seriously come back and report their effects. Others find these prescriptions too onerous. They can't see how these ritualized practices could clarify their vision of themselves or their world.

Rite It Out

If warped rituals have shaped our lives, we must be re-ritualized, oriented to true north. When corrupting rituals have gotten their hooks into us, we act and react. Sometimes the corruption comes from unsafe neighborhoods or abusive homes, which show us that dark ritual honors no socio-economic status. For corrupt rituals, the process is the same: ritual in, expected behavior out. And, of course, children can be the most susceptible to such corruptions.

Children corrupted by dark rituals act out their ritual lives. We're often naïve about this, believing that teaching such children to think differently will make them act better. We believe that if a child understands how her reckless actions affect others, she'll eventually stop misbehaving. But like Vietnam veterans suffering from PTSD, not all children know why they do what they do.

Our church in Newark, New Jersey, spends much of its energy with children from the Newark housing authority neighborhoods. Most people, including the people who live there, would call it "the projects." Many of the kids in that downtrodden neighborhood have been ritualized into appalling practices. Caught in a world ruled by drugs and gangs, these children can't have PTSD because they continue to live in their traumas, never having the opportunity to get to *post*-trauma. In many communities, that's also the case for their parents. These beautiful folks bearing the image of God are often seized by fight-or-flight hypersensitivities.

When we bring our neighbors in for a meal and time together, fights break out over the slightest infractions. These lovely children, by dint of the rituals shaping them and the white noise of violence surrounding them, often lose control of their faculties. And, like a triggered veteran, a child who has reacted violently to nothing more than an antagonistic smirk from another child can't be reasoned with.

After spending years developing friendships in this community, we began to see the world differently. We all remembered watching the now-infamous videos of grown men from similar communities irrationally freaking out and breaking away from police. We used to think, "Why would they do that? They know this isn't going to end well." Now we see our eleven-year-old friends in those videos. Just a few years from now, that could be them. Now we understand that their traumatized bodies react in a way that even they don't understand. It's a mode of panic most of us have never experienced. And years of such violence and uncertainty in a community don't foster rational responses in the moments of their worst crises.

While making friends in that community, we came to realize that if years of community-ritualized violence and uncertainty had burned those reactions into the bodies and minds of those children, then it would take more than a few days or weeks of love and affection to re-orient them.

In the first few years of our friendships with them, we reverted to the standard therapies for misbehavior: talking through what happened, why it was wrong, how it hurt that person, and so on. And reasoning with someone about their misdeeds certainly has its place. But if they're completely overcome by ritualized reactions, they simply can't process such reasoning at that moment.

Most often, a caring hand on the shoulder can be the best immediate response to such episodes. That's no small task when you yourself are upset and pulling apart fighting kids. But research has shown us what we already know: children need regular and appropriate affectionate touch from caring adults. Those who don't get it suffer dramatically over the course of their lives.

Looking at these children as bearers of a "history of rituals" has helped us to appreciate what's great about them and to have patience for what's not so great. Violent or anxious reactions that seemingly come from "out of nowhere" come from somewhere, and can be re-directed toward something better.

If there's one thing the biblical authors are convinced of, it's that we need a new view of reality, one that can envision the reign of God charging into a housing project rife with corruption and the background threat of violence. So we walk alongside these kids, sharing food rituals and offering affection.

There's no easy way to spot when good rituals go bad. And people will always find ways to corrupt rites toward the wrong goals. In fact, we're all using rituals toward our own ends. But unless they have some kind of moral foundation, we will all eventually ritualize our world into a "kingdom of me." These dark rituals don't warn us about "those nefarious folks over there." They warn us about ourselves. We're all prone to bend our rites back in our favor and exploit others in the process.

When this happens, we need other people who care for us to script our rituals. Only they can see us soberly. Only they can help us think about which rituals we must embody and which we must avoid. A caring guide re-ritualizes us out of addiction or violence or whatever our particular darkness is, without twisting us toward their own agendas. It's no accident that the Christian Scriptures describe a wise God who cares for humanity and wants to guide us through rituals for our benefit—no twists, no hooks, no addictions.

Chapter 6

When Rites Go Flimsy

But such men have adapted their falsehood to melodies . . . that by these means they should easily cajole all who read their works.

Philo of Alexandria

"Through my manner of speaking . . . you will feel like you've learned something." These opening words of Will Stephens's TED Talk ironically poke fun at these talks. And his words might be truer than he even realized.

TED Talks landed like a tsunami on the Internet's pop-academic beachfront about a decade ago. If you've never seen a TED Talk, check one out—they're all online and free to watch.[1] TED Talks follow a predictable pattern: a passionate expert delivers a precisely honed, memorable, engaging, and short sermon to a general audience.

When last I checked, the five most-watched TED Talks signal why these monologues are so popular in a culture starving for explanations and answers:

---

1. You can find them at http://www.ted.org/.

"Do Schools Kill Creativity?"
"Your Body Language May Shape Who You Are"
"How Great Leaders Inspire Action"
"The Power of Vulnerability"
"10 Things You Didn't Know about Orgasm"

When I first discovered TED Talks, I loved them. Each one delivers a congenially styled speech by an expert who quickly conveys the skinny on a topic. It doesn't require much effort on the audience's part, either. (Don't worry—TED Talks aren't the villain of my story here; it's just that they represent a style of learning that might accidentally move us away from the fully human use of rituals.)

People enjoy these talks, even if they've progressively become more formulaic as the TED Talk industrial complex has grown. In fact, there now exist at least three TED Talks solely poking fun at the predictable design of the talks. So "parodies of TED Talks" is now a sub-genre of TED Talks.

Infectious by design, TED Talks eventually interjected themselves into our classrooms, but not by our design. Years ago in class, while my students and I were talking through the biblical teaching on poverty relief, a young woman excitedly mentioned that she had seen a TED Talk about the dangers of such efforts. Not much surpasses the beauty of a moment when a student connects the classroom to the outside world. She felt that this twelve-minute speech had transformed her view of poverty relief, and now she heard similar ideas harmonizing in the classroom. We beamed and moved on. So far, so good.

When this kind of comment first started happening, we teachers all understood the excitement over the connection. Many of us had been profoundly affected by one or two TED Talks ourselves. But some of us eventually began to question how a twelve-minute speech could radically transform someone's view of anything at all, especially if transformed understanding is ritualized into us as whole persons over time.

So I started asking more questions when TED Talks came up in conversations. Actually, I would ask just one question: What was the central point of that TED Talk you saw? After all, an expertly focused talk on a single subject should have a memorable point, shouldn't it? The answer to that question took a predictable form: "I don't remember exactly, but it was something about sending shoes to Africa and the local economy being impacted adversely—or something like that."

Despite being fuzzy on the details, all the people I spoke to remembered that they had enjoyed the TED Talk (or speeches like them), and that the expert spoke powerfully. But I wasn't the only one who couldn't quite piece together the significance of any particular TED Talk, and that seemed problematic. (This is when I started falling out of love with TED.)

After hearing such responses numerous times, my colleagues and I began to wonder what most people think happens when they gain a new insight. As professional educators, we have a good grip on the rituals of education, what works and what doesn't. TED Talks, if they indeed transform us, seem to violate what we know to be true about fully human learning.

By "fully human," we mean that the process of education should respect us as entire humans—it should be humane. Humane education respects the time and focused attention required to embody the rites of learning. Now you see why we might want to be wary of smartphone apps as potentially inhumane. Humane education acknowledges the entire *human* person as a learner and the *human* community in which she learns.

My colleagues and I lecture regularly to students, so we're not arguing to end public speaking. And we don't imagine for a second that our lectures create the site of learning. We aren't transferring knowledge to our students. Rather, we try to shape the perspective of their entire persons through the lectures we give, the questions we ask, the discussions, the readings, the essays, the office visits, and more.

Then, inevitably, our students bless us with the gift of seeing things that we ourselves couldn't see. They see the same old texts with fresh eyes, noticing connections obscured to us by our ruts of habit and recycled teaching.

The types of talks that focus on brevity and fluency dress to mimic our humane ways of education, borrowing the trousers and blouses of learning while skimping on the weightier matters of knowledge. We all enjoy the simplicity, engagement, and eloquence of the TED Talk, but those particular garments don't necessarily determine whether we've deeply learned from it.

Dangerous Eloquence

Eloquence packaged in bite-sized talks is nice, but it lacks the key ingredient for transforming our view of reality: time. And quick, well-heeled speeches can cause us to understand less while leading us to believe that we understand more.

In one recent study,[2] researchers showed subjects one of two talks about cat genetics. The two talks contained identical information. However, in the "fluent" version, the speaker had good posture, made eye contact, enunciated well, and had a clearly organized and memorized speech. In the "nonfluent" version, the speaker made all the classic Toastmaster mistakes: "she hunched over a podium, read from notes, spoke haltingly, and failed to maintain eye contact."[3]

One group of subjects saw the *fluent* TED Talk version, and the other group saw the *nonfluent*, stumbling version. After the speeches, researchers quizzed both audiences on the content of

2. Shana K. Carpenter et al., "Appearances Can Be Deceiving: Instructor Fluency Increases Perceptions of Learning without Increasing Actual Learning," *Psychonomic Bulletin & Review* 20, Issue 6 (Dec. 2013): 1350–56; italics mine.

3. Carpenter et al., "Appearances Can Be Deceiving."

the talks they had just heard. They also asked both audiences to estimate how well they thought they did on the quiz.

It might surprise you to learn, as it did me, that both groups scored equally on the content of the talks. Neither style of speech seemed to affect how much the audience learned. But the "fluency" group overestimated how well they did on the quiz. "Thus, students' *perceptions of their own learning and an instructor's effectiveness* appear to be based on lecture fluency *and not on actual learning.*"[4]

The cat's now out of the bag. The eloquent, engaging speaker didn't teach better. Even worse, she left the audience with the impression that they had learned more than they actually did.

Given the prior chapters, we should have seen this train coming. Rhetorical elegance can fool us into believing that we have learned when we were only entranced by the talk's structure and the speaker's skill. Humane rituals that transform our understanding require more of us in both time and energy.

In actuality, when we listen to something like a TED Talk, we don't understand how the subtleties of the topic fit together in a complex relationship. We grasp only the parts of the talk that are cleanly fitted together for us. In the 1960s, Marshall McLuhan once proclaimed, "The medium [the means of communication] is the message." In some ways, something far more pernicious than McLuhan once imagined might occur: *the medium might overthrow the message.*

If this has become the cultural expectation for learning—short, clear, and congenial speeches delivered to a passive audience— then we can see why people like Daniel-*san* resist slow, puzzling, and onerous rituals prescribed by wise guides like Mr. Miyagi. If our families, workplaces, churches, and other groups are the communities that preserve the rituals that transform us, then we might have to sideline certain rituals.

4. Carpenter et al., "Appearances Can Be Deceiving."

For instance, in our churches, workplaces, and schools, we might need to check ourselves when we're impressed by silver-tongued, charismatic leaders. In assessing teaching, how we feel about the message when we hear it can't always be a rule for sound judgment. Let's remember that the most humane instruction of God to Israel came through the blunder-tongued Moses. But God wouldn't allow Moses to recuse himself just because he stumbled in speaking. Maybe God knew something about a truer learning process.

Maybe that learning comes through taking seriously the fact that we generate and improvise rituals in order to see the world more truly. We perform rites to see the kingdom of God in our daily living—from family dinners to diaper changes to staff meetings—not in passive listening.

The Emergency Room and Humane Rituals

Though we find ourselves casually drinking in catchy talks by smooth speakers, our standards for others rise when the stakes are high and the expertise is complex. In many ways, medical doctors have been through those Miyagi-like ritual processes. Because they've embodied those humane rituals, they can see things that we cannot. And we wouldn't tolerate doctors who hadn't listened attentively, embodied their learning, and honed their medical skills through the rituals of medical school.

To make my point, I'll share my own personal story about the time I discovered the magic of medical-school rituals in the skills of an ER doctor. I was twenty-one years old and alone in my car at a stoplight. Suddenly, a bolt of pain struck my upper chest, as if someone had stabbed me to the hilt with a knife. After the initial impact of that stabbing pain, my breathing shallowed and became labored. I focused, laser-like, on each huff of air I could manage. My only thought was "I guess this is how

I'll die." I waited a few seconds for everything to fade to black. But it didn't.

After *not dying* at that stoplight, I drove home. After hours of panting, I called my mother, who was a nurse. I could barely muster enough breath to speak on the phone. She asked me a few questions, then had me bend into certain postures and tell her how I felt in each one. Over the phone and hundreds of miles away, she concluded that I might have a collapsed lung. She insisted that I go to the hospital immediately.

When I came into the emergency room and repeated my mother's diagnosis, the doctor's response was flippant. "If you had a collapsed lung, young man, you wouldn't be sitting here talking to me right now." After sending me off to radiology and waiting until the turn of the century—as ER doctors like to do—he eventually returned with an I'll-be-darned tone to his admission: "Well, it seems that your lung collapsed."

The doctor then popped the black-and-white x-ray film up into the metal clip on the light box. My eyes scanned the x-ray for anything recognizable. The bones were easy enough to make out, but we weren't talking about a single bone on this x-ray. He and I were gathered here together on this day to discuss the lungs inside my rib cage.

This doctor stood beside me, pointing and poking at the film as he explained. As he gestured, he questioned me. "Do you see this thin line here?" He tried to illuminate the x-ray's content to me more than the light box could. Talking and tracing with his finger, he kept at it.

He was almost giddy at what *he* saw, doggedly interrogating me throughout his explanation. "Do you see this mass over here? Do you see this subtle dip in the lung here?" He traced out the signs *for me* that signified *to him* that the lung within my rib cage had collapsed.

How did the doctor know all of this? Because he had been well-schooled in humane medical rituals. And his diagnosis felt humane because he related to me on that level. When rituals are truly humane, we relate to them in all of our humanity—in our ritualed life.

True Vision and Humane Rituals

To become a discerning doctor, a student must listen to her professors in medical school. By dint of tradition and innovations in medicine, medical schools ritualize discernment into the whole being of medical students, not just their minds. Imagine a surgeon whose training consisted entirely of watching surgical videos and reading books. Would we let her operate on us?

In a similar teaching approach, when Jesus puts the disciples under his own training regimen, he tells them to baptize, miraculously heal, supernaturally feed the hungry, and more in order to dispose them to see the "secrets of the kingdom of God." Like medical students, they must listen to him and embody his rites in order to skillfully discern the complexities of the kingdom.

But, against common sense, the disciples rarely listen to Jesus. They do when they are sent out healing. But more often they don't.

When Jesus has compassion on the crowds as sheep without a shepherd, he twice instructs his disciples, "You feed them [the crowds]" (Mark 6:37; 8:4). Both times the disciples don't listen to Jesus, and the Gospel writer then describes the disciples as "hard-hearted" each time (Mark 6:52; 8:17). It's as if Jesus asked them to wax his cars in order to see the secrets of the kingdom of God. Unlike Daniel-*san*, they puzzle, but they don't follow his instructions. So they don't see what Jesus intends them to see.

Ironically, it is outsiders, women, non-Jews, and blind men who seem to see the kingdom most clearly. When Jesus eventually gets fed up with the disciples who aren't listening to him, which is code for "embodying his instructions," he questions their ability to see:

Do you still not perceive or understand?
Have your hearts hardened?
Having eyes, do you fail to see?
Having ears, do you fail to listen?
And do you not remember? (Mark 8:17–18)

What kind of training would have enabled them to see the invisible kingdom that was there the whole time? We never find out in the Gospels. We have to wait until the book of Acts and the New Testament epistles to see clearly how these things fit together.

Today we still use ritualized training, not solely to transfer information, but to dispose ourselves and our students to see something invisible to most, but plain and obvious to those skilled in seeing.

Back in the emergency room, the doctor and I stood together at the precipice of understanding. Could I see all the contours and misshapen bits of lung in the x-ray? No, I could barely recognize any of what he was showing me. But I pretended to understand everything that he said—and I suffered for my arrogance: it only encouraged him to go on in excessive detail.

He saw the object in front of us in a complete and completely different way than I did. It was easy for him to see my lung on the x-ray and to discern its abnormal shape. He visualized the soft pink tissue in three dimensions, now with a flap blown open by some subtle defect. He could chronicle in advance the implications for my life in the coming days and weeks, the new pains and the possibilities of future collapses from scar tissue.

How could he see so much? Here we stood, expert and amateur, discussing my lung, shoulder to shoulder. It was *my* lung, inside *my* body, and I could neither see nor feel the reality he described to me. He might as well have told me that a nymph had taken residence in my lung, poking me from the inside with her wee sword.

He saw in living color the secrets of the kingdom of my internal organs. He saw because his training came humanely, like Daniel-*san*'s: he valued the skills that had been built into his entire body.

Other doctors have since told me that reading x-rays is a skill that comes through precisely one ritual with many variations: looking at a lot of x-rays with an authority over your shoulder who teaches you what to notice and what to disregard.

From learning from Scripture to learning from x-rays, all the components of good knowing come from training by experts who know and script ritual practices over time, which dispose us to see what we could not previously see. Though it is always there before us, we need to perform the rite to know it.

High-stakes professionals understand rituals better than professors in armchairs. Military experts, doctors, firefighters, pilots, and others imbue precise knowledge through ritual, and we wouldn't have it any other way. Who'd get on a plane with a pilot who had only read books about flying?

Our rituals must be humane in the traditional sense. That means we must think about our ethical lives, about how we live, care, buy, plant, and orchestrate our energies. Rituals are humane when they also come from our love for God and our care for others.

Not many of us aspire to be surgeons, but we all want to hone some skill valuable to us. Whether it's knowing the history of punk rock, learning how to successfully parent teenagers, or being able to detect early signs of bipolar disorder, we all seek skilled knowledge in different fields. And in the "field" of faith, the authors of Scripture focus their attention on skilled knowledge as well, returning regularly to processes akin to the training of surgeons. Scripture prescribes embodied practices in order for us to know God, the world, and ourselves rightly.

Our communities grow and flourish when we avoid flimsy pretenders and learn from those who can shape us through humane rituals. For that kind of learning, knowing, flourishing, and depth of confidence to develop, our rites need to look and feel more like surgical training and less like short, smart, three-point talks by smooth communicators. When we learn to question ourselves, holding on to healthy skepticism about ritual practices that only make us feel better about our understanding, that's when we're gathering the tools to dig deeper with mentors. Together we can share rituals, habits, and practices that help us truly flourish in our daily lives, our faith, our vocations and avocations.

RITUALS IN
CHRISTIAN RELIGION

Chapter 7

Getting Some Distance from Our Sacraments

> I have often had a fancy for writing a romance about an English yachtsman who slightly miscalculated his course and discovered England under the impression that it was a new island in the South Seas.
>
> G. K. Chesterton, *Orthodoxy*

When I was a teenager in Tulsa, Oklahoma, my friends and I came across a freakish scene on a walk through the woods. As dusk turned to darkness, we stumbled into a small pocket cleared in the woods. In this clearing, a fire pit held the charred remains of animal bones. Chickens, most likely. The bones were scattered all around, spines twisted unnaturally. Below those bones, someone had scratched a pentagram in the dirt.

We interpreted this as the remnants of an occult animal sacrifice. Remember the 1980s, when everyone was terrified of secret satanic societies stealing children and sacrificing them? Though I wasn't a Christian at the time, Bible Belt culture had wielded sufficient influence over my views of the occult.

So, what had we come across? Was it a sacrament of underground devil-worshipers? Or other teenagers pranking on people walking in the woods? (If it was a prank, kudos to whoever you were.)

Whether sacrifice or stunt, the scene displayed my preconceptions about animal sacrifice: darkness, evil, and secretive ceremonies. It's worth mentioning, though, that Roman citizens accused early Christians of cannibalism. Rumors spread about Christians killing and eating human babies in secret meetings, which didn't endear Romans to those new underground believers.

What's so wrong with chicken-killing rituals in the woods? After all, Christians pretend to eat their god and drink his blood. Jesus even scares away people with the prospect of such a practice. (If you don't believe me, read 6:47–66 in John's Gospel.) You see my point. Even those rituals we don't consider dark and flimsy, those rituals we hold in high regard, are ones we need to consider and truly understand.

Familiar Rites? Rethinking Our Rituals

What we think about Christian sacraments affects how we practice them. If we believe that the waters of baptism wash away the spiritual impurities of sin, then we might start to think about baptism as a regular practice rather than a once-in-a-lifetime act.

Ancient Jewish sects living in Qumran on the Dead Sea did precisely this, incorporating baptisms into their daily rituals. Folks don't usually wander through the Hebrew Bible long enough to realize that baptism descends from the Torah's instructions. *Baptism isn't a New Testament ritual.* Not only is baptism not new to the New Testament; it also gets strategically changed and reutilized within the Hebrew Bible itself.

From the historical washing commands related to the Tabernacle (Exod. 30:18), to the command to wash the bodies of unclean lepers after they were healed (Lev. 14:8), to Elisha's command to Naaman to baptize himself in a river in order to be healed of leprosy (2 Kings 5), the Hebrew Bible offers baptismal rituals that are adapted to particular circumstances.

Then, after the time of the biblical prophets (between 400 BCE to the birth of Jesus), Jewish traditions re-ritualized baptism in several ways, the most popular being a Sabbath ritual called *mikveh* baptism, where Jews descended stairs into stone and plaster baths and then came back up ritually clean.

That Jewish innovation of *mikveh* baptism was then re-ritualized for different purposes by the Dead Sea communities, John the Baptist, John in his baptism of Jesus at the Jordan River, Jesus in the baptism of his followers, and the baptism of the Holy Spirit after Pentecost.

In seeking to understand baptism, we can now see that decoding its symbols won't get us very far. Even within the Bible, those symbols have been reinvested with new meaning. Taking this approach to baptism would be like understanding graduation ceremonies by decoding the symbology of the robes, mortar-board hats, diplomas, speeches, and photo shoots. Just try to think of what graduation robes actually symbolize. (Hint: they descend from seminary rituals.)

If we want to understand the rituals we perform, we must grapple with their lineage, maybe even more than with their possible symbolic meanings. Jesus's strategic modifications of baptism in the New Testament stood in a long line of other forms of baptism, each strategically putting its own twist on previous water rituals. And he didn't just alter baptism; he took an animal sacrifice and made it into the Lord's Supper.

In order to gain a fresh perspective, it's helpful to distance ourselves from our current relationship with the ritual. (No, it's not a breakup—just spending some time apart.) To get to the foundation of baptism, let's first look at the foundation of ritual itself. What are the non-negotiable waypoints of ritual in Scripture? What does a good ritual life look like? How do we know when we've gone overboard or off-kilter? In this chapter we'll begin that exploration and keep asking defining questions in the final two chapters.

Two Rituals: One Strange and One Commonplace

To begin our task of distancing, let's consider two ritual meals. The first may seem strange, and for good reason. The second will be more familiar (at least to those of us in Europe and the Americas).

The Nacirema Ritual

The Nacirema are a nonindigenous tribe still found throughout the Americas. For their primary religious ritual, the Nacirema gather together in a single room once a week. When the people are seated in orderly rows, the leader stands in front of them and commends them to worship their deities, a band of gods connected to an ancient religion from Southwest Asia. Though they sing songs together in honor of these gods, their emphasis on one particular god is unmistakable. The traditional writings of these people include biographies which indicate that the primary god was a charismatic leader, like Hinduism's Krishna, with a large cult following in Southwest Asia.

After finishing their singing and other recitations, the group listens to the leader while he explains the current import of the primitive teachings and encourages those gathered to imitate the cult's ancient leader. Up to this point, the practices seem mostly like large-group activities in their focus on singing, recitation, and listening. However, the memorial ritual at the end of the ceremony draws everyone into direct and intimate participation. It's difficult to observe this ritual without noting how bizarre the practice appears. Based on the primary god's instruction, members act out an incestuous cannibalistic ritual within the group.

Despite the ambiguous roots of the practice, spouses call each other "brother" or "sister" while they consume ritual substances as if they were human flesh and blood. They rip pieces from the ritual flesh and imbibe cups of the ritual blood alongside it. Even some children of the Nacirema participate in the rite. After concluding the ceremony and receiving the leader's blessing, they depart to their homes.

The Congregational Barbeque

Elsewhere in the world, a congregation gathers at a public park in the center of town. As in many such public spaces, barbeque grills and benches indicate the communal and festive nature of the park. Because this community has a shared history, they celebrate with a large picnic for the whole congregation once a year. Each family is responsible for bringing their own food, but they enjoy it together. They begin with a prayer, led by the head shepherd of the group, in which they thank God for everything he has given them, specifically citing how good he has been to them in the past.

Because this town has a special appreciation for such gatherings, the barbeque grills are enormous, able to grill an entire cow if the celebrants so desire. They prepare their food together for several hours, and as dusk gives way to evening, they all eat together as one giant family. The mood is festive, and everyone eats and overeats until they can consume no more. Finally, they depart to their homes.

By now you've probably guessed what I'm doing here. The Nacirema are not an actual tribe. "Nacirema" is "American" spelled backwards. It's an old trick that anthropologists have used to help people think more critically about their own culture, to distance them from that with which they are intimately familiar. The cannibalistic ritual of the Nacirema is usually practiced in church and called Communion, the Eucharist, or the Lord's Supper. It's a ritual that stems from an odd first-century Jewish-Christian practice with which many of us are acquainted.

Let the apparent oddness of the rite sink in for a moment. Communion requires a human sacrifice—Jesus of Nazareth—and includes symbolic cannibalism. Why do people drink wine meant to represent blood? Why do they pretend bread is flesh? If one can see no clear purpose for such a rite, Communion seems like one of the world's most bizarre religious rituals.

Meanwhile, the congregational barbeque is actually a live animal sacrifice practiced on the top of Mount Gerizim in the Palestinian territories of modern-day Israel. The Samaritan people still practice the ancient Hebrew sacrifice of Passover, among other Torah sacrifices, near their temple ruins on the mountain above Nablus (ancient Shechem in the Bible).

When It All Finally Made Sense to Me

The Samaritan Passover, just like the Passover in Exodus, is a rite that requires actual animal sacrifice. In April of 2013, I was able to observe the *Pesach* sacrifice in Kiryat Luza, the small, modern town on top of Mount Gerizim. Several hundred of the world's remaining Samaritan people live next to the ruins of their temple and continue to follow the Samaritan version of Moses's law.

I lived in Jerusalem for a time, investigating the role of rituals in the Bible, so it seemed logical to me to witness a living version of Old Testament animal sacrifice, to splash the sacrificial blood of reality on my imaginings of biblical rituals. A Brazilian friend, bunking with our family at the time, came with me.

On top of Mount Gerizim, dusk had settled in as the spectators thickened around the fenced-off area in the center of town. Surrounded by the typical Israeli concrete-and-stone apartment buildings, the center of Kiryat Luza has an open space, what Europeans would call a plaza. This plaza, however, is of recent vintage: it's a large concrete pad with a basketball court off to one side. On the edge of the plaza, six concrete-coated fire pits sink deep into the ground. In each pit, an orange glow pulses, and flames lick up toward the opening.

That night, thousands of people lined the fenced-off area or climbed on top of the roofs around the plaza. I could feel the mood of the crowd: they were ready for the drama of the killing. As the men of the Samaritan homes brought in the herd of lambs and the high priest made an entrance, the anticipation intensified.

The high priest led the fathers and brothers in recited prayers before preparing the sacrifices. My friend, also an Old Testament professor, and I commented back and forth on what we saw. We tried to compare the men's actions to the Torah's scarce instructions about the Passover sacrifice.

After the prayers ended, the men of each house brought their lamb to the trough that collected the sacrificial blood. As a group, we all intuited when the ritual killing began. Stillness took over. But, despite craning our necks and straining for a view, none of us could see the killing.

The mystery of the sacrifice created by this curtain of Samaritans crowding around only made the strangeness of this seemingly dark practice more pronounced. The killing space was narrow, and we could only see the commotion of the outermost ring of participants. Presumably the butchering occurred in the innermost ring. No flow of blood horrified us, and we spied no animals struggling to live.

Eventually, men posted themselves along the fence at cleaning stations with water spigots. They hosed down the bodies of the de-fleeced lambs, wiping down every animal with their hands.

Then each man took handfuls of coarse salt from a paper bag and rubbed it into the flesh of the animals. As we witnessed this slathering of salt on the lambs, my Brazilian companion turned to me, bewildered. "Churrasco!" he exclaimed. ("Churrasco" basically means "barbeque," and Brazilians barbeque fine cuts of meat by coating them with coarse salt before turning them slowly over a fire.) Clearly, neither of us had previously thought of Passover this way.

As soon as the word "churrasco" left my friend's mouth, it quelled my apprehension of occult sacrifice and the uneasy feeling of sinister darkness that came with it. And then it all made sense to me. *This isn't a secret chicken-killing cult in the woods; it's a giant barbeque! It's a meal. Even more, it's a festival. I practice similar meals in my native culture, too. This isn't cryptic or strange at all.* With that realization, the fourth wall shattered; I was no longer a lingering spectator. Like a movie character who turns to the camera and asks, "Now, how about you?," I felt that the whole bloody ritual was suddenly familiar, intimate.

The mismatch of my expected feelings and the reality that I now witnessed and understood surprised me. On top of Mount Gerizim, I discovered some helpful ways to understand sacrifice and ritual, but, more importantly, I discovered the contours of my artificial boundaries.

What should a person like me expect when crossing over time and religion into a world fluent in ancient and cultic sacrifice? I found myself watching strangely normal human practices exaggerated and specially arranged for this day. After all, every meal with meat that I've ever eaten has also required an animal, sacrificed and butchered on my behalf.

Wesley Bergen observes the irony of our aversion to animal sacrifice: "In our society, . . . we react in horror to the killing of animals, yet happily consume meat in quantities unheard of in the ancient world."[1]

Like a church picnic, this community meal began with prayers, a recognized ritual of many societies. In this case, however, the Samaritans didn't start with pre-packaged meat. Another, more striking difference was that Passover in this place was a normal activity—a community barbeque—ritualized around a particular historical event: Israel's exodus from Egypt.

---

1. Wesley Bergen, "Studying Ancient Israelite Ritual: Methodological Considerations," *Religious Compass* 1, no. 5 (2007): 579–86.

In truth, this ritual differs significantly from what occurs in butcher shops or at festive church picnics of American fare. And, contrary to what we might think, it's not the animal killing that distinguishes it, though live animal sacrifice might be most distracting to those trying to visualize it. Rather, we discover the true difference of this ritual when we ask a set of important questions:

Who scripted this ritual?
What is the goal of the ritual?
Who must practice it?
What is necessary to perform the ritual, and what can be improvised?

As we've seen before, Exodus states the purpose of Passover in plain language: *this* ceremony imbues *this* day with particular memories of Israel's exodus from the house of slavery in Egypt. The holy day exists to teach children about God's intervention on behalf of Israel, and to do so in a way that makes it personal for them: "For on this day, I [God] brought you all out of the land of Egypt" (Exod. 12:17). The purpose of the festival is to instill in these children a correct and living memory of those events and of history itself.

If Jews just recited the facts of Israel's history or gave their children a book to read, then their children would have a set of mere facts. But the author of Exodus presumes that the entire ceremony is not for the mere remembering of facts, but is meant for the correct understanding of what happened from an embodied and communal perspective.

Memorials in Scripture—its ceremonies, rituals, and monuments—are specifically created so that children will learn the importance of key events through their parents' guidance. Memorials are not about curiosity but about the communal classroom that shapes a people's knowledge of itself and the world over time.

The Thicker Life of Rituals

Commemorating past events pervades Western culture even now. Birthdays, anniversaries, and national holidays offer us a taste of what happens in biblical rituals. But these celebrations are flimsy guides to understanding the ritualed world as we meet it in Scripture. At best, our cultural memorials are often just that: reminders of past events. At worst, holidays such as birthdays morph into celebrations oddly focused on only one of the people involved in the birth: the child.

With a different lens, Moses and Jesus frame Israel's rites as guides for seeing the world soberly. Practicing rites in a community fosters an ability to see and understand. This makes sense of that cryptic phrase in Deuteronomy proclaiming that God's instructions—which include Israel's rituals—"will be your wisdom and your understanding in the sight of the peoples, who, when they hear all these statutes, will say, 'Surely this great nation is a wise and understanding people'" (Deut. 4:6).

It often isn't clear to us how embodying rituals such as upholding ethical standards and caring for the poor and the immigrant can make us wise. Unless those rituals are more than merely symbolic expressions, performances to make us feel better, or placebo-like actions that prove our trust in God, then it's difficult to see how they create wisdom. Yet the prophets insist that God's instruction teaches Israel how to be and how to see *through her rituals*. And the wisdom to be gained from thinking through these ritual principles together might also be a worthy pursuit.

If we're honest, we admit that it's not immediately clear how scriptural laws and teachings about crime, animal sacrifice, and ritual cleansing form an adequate classroom for wisely understanding all of reality. How does a Passover ritual guide Hebrews to know the world differently? Does it reveal something crucial they would otherwise be blind to?

Yes, actually. It's similar to the purpose of the ritualized practice you're participating in as you now peruse this page. We call this ritual "reading a book," in which someone attempting to be a guide shows you something you haven't seen before or appreciated in quite the same way. At the very least, the bodily rite involves your hands, eyes, brain, time, and mental energies. At most, it allows you to grapple with different concepts and visualize ritual scenes in order to create connective tissue between the relationships being drawn together.

The basic process in Hebrew ritual is at work here: a guide (albeit an imperfect one) shares insight and hopes to guide you toward it, to enable you to see it for yourself, metaphorically speaking. As a reader, you embody the ritual practice of reading attentively and ignoring myriad distractions in order to participate in a process of learning.

We might even call a book like this the ritual artifact, the memorial stone that requires a response. You will bring questions to this book that are prompted by the practice of reading it. Its pages are like the stone monuments at the Jordan River, the blood splashed on the altar, or the wine of the Lord's Supper. None of these instill discernment in and of themselves, but they do act as the instruments of our understanding—like the biologist's microscope or the social scientist's experimental data. We don't stare *at the microscope* in order to discern something about the cells in the glass slides. We look *through the microscope* to see what it can show us.

We best understand the meaning of the rituals in the Hebrew Bible and the New Testament when we discern *through them*, not by staring at them, dissecting them, or decoding them as symbolic acts. Which brings us back to Passover. When Israel's children eat roasted lamb at a large community meal and listen to their parents' interpretations of its significance, these acts focus the lens through which they truly see the world and history and their place in both.

Through Scripture and the rituals we find there, Moses and Jesus function as our guides. Through them we begin to learn that the use of rituals is not only good for biblical instruction, but reflects the best learning approach in the enterprises of science, parenting, teaching, coaching, counseling, managing, and so on. In this regard even the most apparently bizarre rituals become familiar to us because our lives are already deeply ritualed—from learning chemistry to fostering virtue to planning church picnics to observing holidays—and yes, even pressing the elevator "Close Door" button.

Where We Go from Here

So, what makes Christian rituals "Christian"? And where do we begin to understand how to revise rituals while keeping them Christian in their grounding? As with jazz and comedy, revision and improv flow from an intimate knowledge of scales, riffs, and characters. And improvisation requires practice that springs from foundational work.

With Christian rituals, we improvise, but how do we judge that improvisation? What if we use Doritos and Mountain Dew for Communion?

We will explore the boundaries of our ritual improvisations soon enough. But I would be remiss if I didn't first point out the gigantic elephant in the room: the intricate biblical connections between our everyday morality and the rituals we perform.

Chapter 8

Avoiding the Ethical Rift

Hear this word,
you cows of Bashan [aka Israelite lady-folk] . . .
who oppress the poor,
who crush the needy . . .
Bring your sacrifices every morning,
your tithes every three days;
Bring a thank offering of leavened bread,
and proclaim freewill offerings, publish them;
For so you love to do, O people of Israel!
    says the Lord Yahweh.

                    Amos the prophet (Amos 4:1, 4–5)

So when you are offering your gift at the altar, if you remember
that your brother or sister has something against you, leave
your gift there before the altar and go; first be reconciled to
your brother or sister, and then come and offer your gift.

            Jesus, Sermon on the Mount (Matt. 5:23–24)

Sacraments don't begin in the church. They begin in what we do
and say—in our homes, with our phones, on our computers, at
our jobs, through our shopping habits. They are expressed when

we invest in others, when we offer our power for the sake of the powerless, and more. Remember what made the sacrament of placebos effective: the ethical treatment from a caring physician combined with a ritual. The effectiveness of the sugar-pill ritual flowed from the doctor's concern for the patient *as a human* into the daily rituals of the patient at home. So rituals and our daily lives connect, ever entwined together.

In the epigraphs that begin this chapter, we read the warnings of Amos and Jesus. In both cases, they presume that people perform the Torah festivals and sacrifice rituals as they should. If we could travel back in time and watch these Hebrews through a closed-circuit TV camera, it would all look religiously up to snuff. Yet God rejected their ritual offerings for one reason: because there was no meaningful connection to their treatment of neighbors, strangers, the poor, and others.

Because those biblical women in Bashan oppressed the poor in the days of Amos, they invalidated the import and meaning of their ritual sacrifices. And their mistreatment of others did more than contaminate their offerings. Unbeknownst to them, their immoral behavior also blinded them to God's purposes for them—made them dumb and numb to the world God was trying to show them.

It was the same in Jesus's day, when he was desperately trying to show his contemporaries how to live out the kingdom of God. He taught his disciples a radical but ancient prophetic command. When someone had a beef against a fellow Jew and tried to offer a sacrifice in the Temple, Jesus said, "Leave the sacrifice!" The trouble needed to be mended before the Temple rituals were done (Matt. 5:24). The point is clear: How you treat folks makes your rituals acceptable as a fragrant aroma to God—or rejected as a foul stench.

A Wise and Discerning People

In teachings across the Bible, the more we notice the prophets' integration of the moral life with the ritualed world, the more we see the rift in our own ethical lives in our Christian circles today. How we build our houses (Deut. 28:2), treat the immigrant (Lev. 19:34), treat the thief who robs our house (Exod. 22:2–3), and treat animals (even the animals of our "enemies") changes the very nature of our rituals in God's eyes—and nose (Exod. 23:4).

We might recall the original stated purpose of this ritualed world that Israel entered: living out the ethical ritual life would inevitably lead to outsiders exclaiming, "Surely this great nation is a wise and discerning people" (Deut. 4:6).

When we look at the gulf between what we say we believe and how we live—from the way we treat our waiter to the way we incarcerate lawbreakers—we may realize that the non-negotiable ritual morality given in Scripture has fallen by the wayside for us. We would do better to heed Scripture and recognize that what God has joined together—ethical behavior and rituals—let no one tear apart.

In the New Testament, the apostle Paul teaches the Corinthian church to check themselves before they wreck themselves when it comes to their moral behavior before rituals (1 Cor. 11). If they bicker with each other, then they need to evaluate whether their ritual participation can be acceptable. Paul even connects Passover as a festival they should celebrate, but he tweaks the tradition so that Jesus is the Passover lamb, and the people have prepared for the ritual with their moral lives (1 Cor. 5:6–8). (Paul also has to warn the Corinthian Christians to quit having sex with their stepmoms and getting drunk on the Communion wine. Clearly these are real people with real problems.)

Of course, an emphasis on morally preparing for rituals can also go too far. In the Church of Scotland, some parishes would serve Communion only twice a year. In between those bi-annual

Lord's Suppers, elders visited all the houses in their parish to verify that parishioners were sufficiently penitent in preparation for the Communion service. If the family passed muster, then the elder gave them a Communion coin, which they brought to church. Imagine—needing a coin, a form of payment, to take Communion! Because their culture's moral code demanded such great contrition from believers, some parishes couldn't enjoy the blessing of more frequent Communion.

Whatever practices we narrow down to, we can't maintain an ethical rift that separates moral behavior from the rituals of Christianity. How we engage others at home, at work, and in the marketplace *is* part and parcel of our so-called spiritual life. And the ritual principles outlined in Scripture can guide us and allow us to improvise without falling into dark and flimsy rites—compromising our morality and wisdom.

Scripture concentrates its attention not on individual practices but on community practices that draw on what Jesus calls "the mystery of the kingdom of God" (Mark 4:11) and what Paul calls "hidden wisdom from God" (1 Cor. 2:7). And so we find Jewish and Christian traditions prescribing embodied actions, such as caring for those on the fringes of society, in order to create a certain type of wise community.

Not only do the Torah and Jesus prescribe embodied practices for the sake of wisdom; they also prohibit certain practices that detract from wisdom. Exploitative practices, such as visiting prostitutes or holding onto a poor man's wages, become crimes against God and the earth. Such crimes actually pollute the land beneath their feet, to use the language of the Hebrew Bible, and their wickedness dulls their discernment—as wrongdoing tends to do. The wisdom writer sums it up best: "The way of the wicked is like deep darkness; they do not know over what they stumble" (Prov. 4:19). The ritualed world of Scripture aims precisely at our discernment—a wise kind of seeing fostered in the community of God's people.

Be Afraid, Be Slightly Afraid

Now we know. Looking out for the vulnerable in their society was part of Israel's ritual occupation. And all the prophets felt free to call out Israel when she transformed from the oppressed to the oppressor—especially Amos. And just as God heard the cries of the Hebrews being oppressed in Egypt, God also heard the cries of those suffering under Israelite oppression. On behalf of God, Amos warned Israel, "Because you trample the poor and tax grain from him . . . " (5:11),

> I hate, I despise your festivals,
> and I take no delight in your solemn assemblies.
> Even though you offer me your burnt offerings and grain
>   offerings,
> I will not accept them. . . .
> Take away from me the noise of your songs;
> I will not listen to the melody of your harps.
> But let justice roll down like waters,
> and righteousness like an ever-flowing stream.
>
>   (Amos 5:21–24)

The language of Jesus is no less harsh:

> Not everyone who says to me, "Lord, Lord," will enter the kingdom of heaven, but only the one who does the will of my Father in heaven. On that day many will say to me, "Lord, Lord, did we not prophesy in your name, and cast out demons in your name, and do many deeds of power in your name?" Then I will declare to them, "I never knew you; go away from me, you evildoers."
>
>   (Matt. 7:21–23)

It's as if Jesus could sense our attempts to find a workaround, and he cuts off all our routes in advance. Try as we might, we can't

107

avoid his message—or the truth of our behavior. If we're honest, we don't want our treatment of the earth, the animals, and others to make our Christian rituals foul or fragrant to God.

But our regard for this world we inhabit on Tuesday night fuses with and manifests itself in the rites we strategically embody on Sunday morning—for good or for ill. We can see the choices that God has set before us today: We can be an ethically wise and ritualized community, or we can choose behaviors that create a great rift of ethical hypocrisy, dumbing and numbing us to the hidden wisdom of God. We might want to think about which path our communities have typically chosen and why.

And we can find inspiration in the fine communities that exemplify ethical wisdom. I think of Henri Nouwen's renowned work in the L'Arche community as a superb example. Their mission statement says it best:

> We are people, with and without intellectual disabilities, sharing life in communities belonging to an International Federation. Mutual relationships and trust in God are at the heart of our journey together. We celebrate the unique value of every person and recognize our need of one another.[1]

Living daily alongside people who face a variety of cognitive and physical challenges must culminate in rich worship rituals for all on Sunday. Certainly the wisdom of everyone in the community grows through these mutually beneficial relationships. The old model of the church as messianic savior—we are here to help the hurting—has been questioned in past decades because of communities such as L'Arche that demonstrate the full integration of a biblically ethical community and rituals of worship. And as a community of people with mixed abilities, L'Arche teaches everyone in that community about the kingdom of God. What a wise and discerning people.

1. https://www.larcheusa.org/who-we-are/charter/.

The Medical School Model:
Developing Wisdom and Discernment

It's not just religious communities that connect ethics and ritual practices for the purpose of developing discernment. The community of surgeons who script the rituals of surgical skill is the same community who later certifies successful students as "surgeons."

What view of ethics animates a medical community that is designed to impart the technical wisdom of medicine? According to the Hippocratic Oath, written in the fourth century BCE, medical practice is oriented toward the health of a community through its individuals. To that end, it is humane in its training, which engages the whole person within community, and humane in its goal of community health:

- Whoever I visit, rich or poor, I will concern myself with the well-being of the sick. I will commit no intentional misdeeds, nor any other harmful action such as engaging in sexual relations with my patients (regardless of their status).
- Whatever I hear or see in the course of my professional duties (or even outside the course of treatment) regarding my patients is strictly confidential and I will not allow it to be spread about. But instead, will hold these as holy secrets.

That's right—physicians in antiquity actually had to say it out loud: I won't have sex with my patients. Think about what that presumes: rituals that ingrain a keen understanding of illness can be fouled by the abuse of power or privilege. The oath also presumes that a physician's ethical life makes her analyses, judgments, and ritual surgical practices fragrant, not foul.

Surgical training is inherently ethical—some might say moral. On a good day, surgical education aims at producing people who can consistently answer this fundamental question: Should I strategically harm this person's body in surgery in an effort to make them whole? After answering that question, more ensue. Do I have the surgical discernment to humanely perform the operation? Am I perversely motivated to act because of money or a naïve messiah complex? More questions like these can be asked, but you get the idea. We have to ethically train discernment into our surgeons, and that isn't a modern approach.

Note that we don't send our children off to medical *yogis* or *senseis* to study under only one surgical master. An entire community must be dedicated to establishing the ways in which surgeons can and cannot learn their vocation. That's why we commend students to medical colleges, where colleagues script rituals meant to humanely form students in their skilled discernment.

In medical colleges, students and professors practice interpretation of the texts of surgical literacy in deep community: reading x-rays, processing lab results, examining patients, and so on. And only through the skilled guidance of that community can students learn to treat patients in ways that have been ritualized into them.

Like the world of surgery, where ethical practices lie at the heart of every part of surgical rituals, the moral life of Christians is meant to be fully integrated so that everything we touch, do, think, and say is fully connected to our ability to see what God is showing us.

Our world is ritualed, which means that the sacraments we perform within our faith communities throughout the calendar year are *funded from* the poverties we relieve in our larger communities. If rituals shape our understanding of the world, then everything we do morally prepares our rites as well—for good or for ill. The ritualed world prescribed in Scripture and practiced in our best instances of skilled understanding—such as the modern medical community—operates best when it operates humanely. Like surgeons, we need to live in a wise community that tests and critically assesses our understanding against the fairest standard of all: the health of the body of Christ and its members.

Chapter 9

Riting Our Wrongs

To state the facts frankly is not to despair the future nor indict the past. The prudent heir takes careful inventory of his legacies and gives a faithful accounting to those whom he owes an obligation of trust.

John F. Kennedy

Sincere but Misdirected Ritual

Believe it or not, it is possible for thousands of folks healed from blindness to sincerely and zealously praise the wrong people for their new sight. A 2007 National Geographic documentary follows a Nepalese eye surgeon invited to North Korea to perform as many cornea replacements as he can in just ten days.[1] On this humanitarian mission, the surgeon also trains North Korean doctors to continue his work once he's gone. Over a thousand functionally blind persons become sighted in a matter of days.

1. National Geographic Explorer, "Inside North Korea," season 21, episode 14 (February 27, 2007).

When the medical staff finally removes their bandages, most of these patients see clearly for the first time in decades. The moment is expectedly emotional. Weeping and displays of gratitude overtake them. Women and men alike bow low in gratefulness. Some even sing songs. Others lead the whole multitude of previously blind patients in chants and cheers, even grandiose hymns of praise.

As the camera turns to their object of praise, their behavior immediately ceases to make sense. The newly sighted masses direct none of their thanksgiving to the surgeon or his team. Instead, they direct all glory and honor to the paintings of the then-current and former leaders of the People's Republic of Korea: Kim Jong-il and his father. The paintings deafly and mutely receive the praise.

The patients' religious devotion to the leaders of their country clouds their ability to see *who* has done *what* for them. Through the camera lens, the documentarian not so subtly indicates for viewers the rightful recipients of the praise: the surgical team who voluntarily came to restore sight.

These acts of worship and loyalty might appear absurd to us, but such actions reveal the cancerous nature of badly prescribed rituals. Kim Jong-il had reportedly ritualized sycophantic worship into the culture over decades. Such blind worship would need to be "ritualized out" over time so that worshipers could understand the gross misdirection of their devotion. Of course, even our disdain for North Korea's regime stems from a system of disgust that's been ritualized into us through the Western way of seeing things. All versions of what makes a good ritual "good" are not equal, but some version of the story is always ritualizing us.

Twenty seven hundred years before this, Israel's ritual adultery to Ba'al looked like a similar insanity to the prophets. Out of her desperate need for water and her mistrust of God, Israel became God's prodigal wife. Hebrews gave the fruit of their fields to Ba'al, a local fertility god, instead of Yahweh, their God.

According to the prophets, their rituals to Ba'al blinded them from seeing that it was Yahweh who sent the rains on the land. Like the ritualized North Koreans praising the mute images of their leaders, Israel took gifts from Yahweh and offered them up to Ba'al. Through Hosea, God bluntly addresses Israel's distorted vision:

> She [Israel] did not know
> that it was I [Yahweh] who gave her the grain, the wine, and
>   the oil,
> and [I] who lavished upon her silver and gold that they used
>   for Baal. (2:8)

In her mixed worship of both the god of Canaan and the God of Israel, she became dull to reality. Like the pit digger from Proverbs who falls into his own pit, Israel finds even God's instruction to her to be a stumbling block because of her misguided ritual practices. The final words of the prophet startle us with a sobering view. Our ritualed lives, not just our world of thoughts, determine whether God's instruction will guide us to flourish or will become the petard upon which we hoist ourselves:

> Those who are wise understand these things . . .
> and the upright walk in them,
> but transgressors stumble in them. (Hos. 14:9)

Taking Stock

The brutal reality of Israel's lesson repeats over and over throughout the Scriptures. Undiscerning people become deadened to reality by the ritual lives they've constructed. When they encounter God's loving guidance, they see it as a hurdle to be overcome rather than a path to be walked with gratitude.

Clearly, being sincere or zealous isn't enough. Israel was zealous in the days of Hosea and later in the days of Jesus. But how can we know if we're zealously wrong? To truly begin to discern, we need to ask and answer difficult questions like these:

- Have we mistaken the gifts of God for well-earned salaries and the privileges that they afford?
- Do the palpably repetitive biblical themes of divestment, humility, servitude to others, and foolishness for the sake of this good news interfere with our consumerist ritual pursuits?
- Do we glide through the parts of Scripture that affirm God's love for us and stumble over the rituals required to understand the kingdom of God and to embody it on earth?

To think through these questions, we might begin with an inventory of our ritualed lives—as individuals, as families, as coworkers, and as the church. (See the appendix for an example of this inventory.) We might think of it in terms of a spending problem. If we habitually spend too much money, financial planners don't start by saying, "Stop overspending!" Almost counterintuitively, they start with an inventory, keeping track of every penny in and out of our bank accounts. Their strategy is smart, because once we know how we spend our money, we can begin to think about correcting our spending or improving its effectiveness.

The following questions provide a structure for taking inventory of our ritualed world and reflecting on our answers:

1. *Inventory*: What rituals do we currently embody (daily, weekly, yearly), and what are their effects?
2. *Authorities*: Who or what primarily scripts those rites (culture, tradition, Scripture)?
3. *Safe Practice*: How do we move safely from instruction to wise practice and informed improvisation?
4. *Rites Gone Wrong*: In what way could our ritual life lean toward

dark and flimsy ritualization? Stated otherwise: How can these rites turn inhumane?

Taking Ritual Inventory

If rituals are normal practices strategically changed for some other purpose, then we need to inventory the singular events of our lives and our habitual practices. These should give us a good view of what we're doing and why. What kinds of things do we do only once in a lifetime, and what practices do we embody daily, monthly, and yearly?

Daily Rituals

Among the questions we might ask ourselves in inventory mode, here's a particularly important one: Does my day have a discernible rhythm? If not, why not? If so, what determines that rhythm? Is the rhythm purely reactionary, entirely devoted to picking up kids or making meetings on time? Who do I know that structures their daily rhythms well?

If we're being honest, here are two of the questions a lot of us ask ourselves. How did our days end up enslaved to the demands of bosses, friends, and our own desires? And how is it that we spend so much time shuffling our kids to all these activities, and yet we seem to have lost touch with them? There's a genuine reckoning to be had about the frenetic pace of our children's after-school events.

But we can ritualize these moments as well. Instead of being just a car ride to practice, it could be a time to listen to a musician's song and think critically together about the lyrics. We could also suggest topics to think about for future discussions. ("I want you to think about the lives of people ten years after they're no longer famous and what that would be like for them. What kind of wisdom do you think they'd have for us?")

These aren't rituals that we're making from scratch: we're actually thinking about how to improvise the command to instruct our children about God. Deuteronomy 6 famously commands Israel to love God, but also commands parents to teach our children about what God has done for us at all these little intersections of life—as we drive to practice, as we share a meal, as we get ready for bed, and so on.

For instance, there's something profoundly rich in thinking with our children—or our friends or our parents—about why the Torah commands us to love the immigrant and to not let them fall into poverty. Or why the son of God would take the time to teach us not to swear oaths. And what does this mean for us? What kind of people would we be and how would society work if no one ever had to promise by contract to do anything?

Our daily rituals usually take place in three particular "spaces" of time.

The Morning Hustle: Waking up, getting cleaned up and dressed, eating breakfast, and commuting consume most of our early mornings. We all have sluggards in the family, and in deference to the lowest common denominator, most families aim at efficiency rather than elegance in these early hour rites—as long as they get us all up and ready, we're generally OK with them. Most morning routines are geared toward getting us somewhere we're actually interested in being for the day. (Unless we loathe our jobs or school, in which case we might savor the preamble to our day.)

Working Hours: Do our labors bring us into contact with the real world and offer satisfaction? Hard, repetitive jobs force the question of meaning. But even if we achieve our dream job, after the initial thrill has dulled, we might step back and wonder: *What am I doing? What difference does any of this make?*

Psalm 1 describes the flourishing person as someone who "delights in the Torah and meditates on it day and night." "Meditate" here implies mulling over and embodying the instruction of God in everything we do—whether that's preparing annual budgets, breaking up concrete, teaching the ABCs, or plowing a field. The bold presumption by the biblical author goes something like this: God's instructions have something to say about everything we do.

Thinking through Scripture's teaching while doing all we need to do in the world ritualizes our day's work so that we can see reality better—understand how our work makes meaningful contact with the kingdom of God. Or maybe this reflection shows us that our work can't fit into the kingdom. And then we have a different kind of work to do.

The Evening Gathering: Unless you're living alone, the evening re-gathers the troops back at home. Having a place we call home and the gathering rituals associated with it are critically important to the health of families.

In fact, every ritual can have lasting significance. John Gottman's research on family rituals has shown that how spouses treat each other when they leave in the morning and re-connect at night can have a great impact on their marriage over the years. Making it a priority to have distraction-free, physical acknowledgment of our spouses in the morning and again at night—perhaps with a hug and a kiss—has life-long effects for both parents and children.[2]

Just imagine the difference in how we might understand humanity if we never saw our parents act affectionately towards each other or us. How we leave each other and greet each other, how we gather for our evening meal, and how we settle in at night—all these rituals not only prepare us for the next day but shape our relational sense of ourselves and others.

2. The Gottman Institute Blog is a rich resource for evidence-based articles on family life and marriage. See https://www.gottman.com/blog/.

Weekly (Shabbat-ly) Rituals

The seven-day structure of our week comes from the creation story found in the Hebrew Bible, where God worked six days and rested on the seventh. In our zealousness, we doubled down on the biblical command to rest, and now we act as though a two-day weekend is just a normal part of life. But it's not. Only people as posh as *Downton Abbey*'s Dowager could be so bold as to ask unironically, "What is a weekend?"

For most of the world throughout most of history, seven days of work per week was the norm. Only Hebrews and some Christians would work six days and rest on the seventh. Ancient Roman elites took note of this Jewish practice and scoffed at it as laziness.

Putting a big 24-hour pause in each week was a bold move for God. It separated those who truly trusted God from those who faked it. Some have even argued that the notion of human rights entered the world only through the idea of Sabbath. In the ancient Near East, only Israel considered animals, servants, Hebrews, and immigrants as equals one day a week. The whole motley crew rested together.

Sabbath was practiced by the earliest followers of Jesus—apostles like Paul, Peter, James, and the others. They still took time on the first day (Sunday) to gather at the Temple in Jerusalem.

Like the end-of-day gatherings in our homes, the re-gathering of God's people every Sabbath took on more importance the further away from Jerusalem they lived. The apostles used these Sabbath gatherings as the hubs for their missions to the world. Paul and the writer of Hebrews insisted on continuing these gatherings as evidence that the church functions like a body, which needs all of its members.

The Sabbath principle is still supposed to be at the heart of the modern Christian world. When it comes to Sabbath, I don't know what surprises modern Christians more: that we're still expected to keep some kind of Sabbath practice, or that God still commands us to work six (not five) days a week.

But it's the usual suspects who write the ritual scripts for our weekends. Leisure-product manufacturers, party supply stores, and upscale grocery stores dole out enticing scripts for the "ultimate weekend." The travel and hotel industry prescribe the "ultimate weekend getaway." Wineries and breweries have jumped into this high-stakes game as well. Loverboy's assessment that "everybody's working for the weekend" still rings true. On the other side, the American drive to succeed and prove ourselves at work hits us in another soft spot: workaholism.

Whether it's enticements to play or inducements to work, dark and flimsy versions of Sabbath surround us, and discernment on how to ritualize our weekly rhythms doesn't come easy. But the primacy placed on re-gathering with God's people and the metaphor of rest always associated with the Sabbath must have some prescriptive force in our weekly rituals.

Annual and Occasional Rituals

We know that all Christians in the early church celebrated Easter, and that Jesus commanded us to celebrate other rituals like the Lord's Supper. But the birth of Jesus was not celebrated—either by Jesus or his apostles. And we read about Jesus's birth in only two of the four Gospels. Still, we celebrate the birth of Jesus every year.

But are we really doing that—or have the commercial attractions of Christmas completely overtaken our remembrance of Christ? We should give some careful thought to our Christmas rituals and what effect they have on us. What might we be able to do to change this?

We all know of the Christmas gift rituals that powerfully overtake a child's entire being year after year. And how about the Santa Claus myth? I couldn't even convince my own young children that Santa Claus didn't exist because every kid in their school believed it so vigorously. Even worse, most of the adults around them re-inforced this "strategic untruth."

For our family, simplifying Christmas has helped. Giving fewer gifts and stretching the December 25 holiday into the season of Advent has helped, too. But it's a tough row to hoe because parents everywhere are ritualizing Christmas into their kids, no matter what kind of Christmas they choose to observe.

True, many churches now celebrate Advent as a way of remembering Christ's coming as well as his birth. Still, "American Christmas" seems to win our hearts and wallets and time and attention.

And we have other traditional annual celebrations besides Christmas—Easter being the primary one. But has our celebration of Christ's resurrection been co-opted by the Easter bunny, the Easter ham, and our plans for spring break? We may have traditions for both of these special times—but how meaningful are they? What rituals are we employing, and why? Or have we reached the point where we're simply going through the motions, merely repeating things that we've done all our lives? These are questions we should ask about non-religious celebrations too—Thanksgiving, anniversaries, birthdays, and more.

When we take a close and thoughtful inventory of these rituals, we realize that we may have some work to do. If a bad rite has made its way into our ritualed world, we just might have to ritualize it out.

Who's Prescribing Our Rites?

In Christian Scripture, rituals aim at the health of the community and the individuals within it. A rising tide lifts all boats. This won't always mean a pain-free existence, as Jesus promises suffering and poverty as real possibilities for those who follow him. But it will mean that individual lives and the communal life of the church will be immeasurably enriched and deepened.

Rites come from all sorts of places—families, friendships, jobs, churches, and our surrounding culture. In my ritual inventory (see the appendix), I consider who wants me to do something and what rituals they prescribe to achieve their ends. When I take this inventory, my goal isn't to emancipate myself from rituals, but to consider the often perverse incentives in performing what others prescribe. All of us do these inventories, and though our rites may differ, the bottom-line question for all of us is the same: Who should write our rituals? Who should prescribe them? And how should we assess them?

Just because a ritual is thousands of years old, for instance, doesn't make a ritual good. And it might not even be thousands of years old.

If you've ever taken a yoga class (or learned yoga through Nintendo's Wii Sports like I did), then you'll know the downward-facing dog, the lotus, and other positions practiced to increase strength and flexibility. We're often told that this is a centuries-old form of exercise.

But if you've ever taken a world religions class, you'll know that the Hindi word *yoga* doesn't refer to a specific set of stretches, but to ascetic disciplines of all sorts in the Hindu religion. Spiritual teachers called *yogis* commend various *yogas*—from sexual practices (think the *Kama Sutra*) to wrestling to extreme fasting—to train practitioners to understand genuinely difficult concepts within Hinduism.

Michelle Goldberg's research shows that one yogi brought a specific yoga from India to America and turned this yogic ascetic practice into a form of exercise.[3] The only wrinkle is that Indra Devi—born Eugenie Peterson—was not an ancient yogi but an entrepreneurial writer who traveled to India in the early twentieth century. And, based on what she learned there, she invented most

---

3. Michelle Goldberg, http://www.npr.org/sections/health-shots/2015/06/01/411202468/those-yoga-poses-may-not-be-ancient-after-all-and-maybe-thats-ok.

of the positions of modern yoga. (Indian yogis reportedly do not know where these positions and their names came from.)

Traditionally, one of yoga's appeals has been its ancient and sagacious Indian roots. But now we find out that an enterprising modern woman invented this specific style of yoga and pawned it off as an old Hindu practice. Of course, this doesn't diminish the health benefits of yoga. But it reminds us that, as with all exercises (and religions), it's important to know what roots ground the ones who prescribe rituals to us.

Whether they're the liturgies of church services or stretching exercises taught to us by physical therapists, getting rituals right inherently involves a process of critique. Our evaluation focuses on the one who claims authority to prescribe rituals to the community. Why do we trust the prescriber? Do they have enough knowledge and experience to understand how this rite works? Do they know how it can turn dark or flimsy, and how it how it can be reclaimed?

When we're evaluating our rituals, Christian or otherwise, we need to remember the three categories of ritual prescribers:

Routine (daily necessities create habits that prescribe rites)
Tradition (skilled persons and traditions prescribe rites)
God (divine command and tradition prescribe rites)

In all cases, rituals have necessary parts and elements of improvisation. When we're considering who prescribes a rite, it's important to think about what constitutes a proper improvisation of the rite. For instance, the Hebrew Bible and the New Testament affirm charitable giving as a fundamental ritual of God's people. Some giving is specifically instructed, such as peace offerings, but other giving rituals, such as almsgiving, are prescribed without directions. Here we need a clear grasp of charity and poverty in the Hebrew Bible in order to understand Jesus's intention when he commends giving. This understanding will inform our improvisation.

Understanding who prescribes a ritual *and to what end* determines how we practice the rite and when we alter it. With Christian ritual, the goal is to practice the rites to know God, his kingdom, his creation, and his creatures truly—avoiding the blind worship described earlier. To do this well, we must consider what is clearly required in our ritual lives and how to improvise with wisdom.

Chapter 10

Practicing Safe Ritual Improvisation

> Learn the rules and then break them in such a way as to exercise good taste.
>
> Sir George Shearing

"Safety" isn't a word we typically associate with rituals. But I'm scared scriptless about rituals going sideways on us. Dark, flimsy, or blindly performed rites that are despised by God ought to scare us. And let's face it: rites can easily go wrong, and they have for all of us in one or more areas of our lives.

Up to this point we've been thinking about rituals as a formative part of our lives. We've investigated the ritual-makers and how we should assess them. But we also need to make sure that we're performing our rituals—especially our sacred rituals—rightly. Which brings up this question: How do we know when we've violated the very point of the rites given by God through the prophets?

In the end, it's less important to figure out what rituals *are* than to think about faithfully embodying the rites of Scripture as individuals within a community. We need to remember that Christian rites can't merely act like defunct "Close Door" elevator buttons, just there to give us a false sense of control. We also know that we can't enact these rites as if we're taking placebo pills, giving performances merely meant to demonstrate our trust in the prescriber. And we can't enact them as merely symbolic expressions of our inner authentic selves, like parables needing to be decoded.

Rituals function in all of these ways and more, but focusing on rituals as symbols, performances, or therapies alone yields a flimsy scheme for reflecting on such bounty. Now we can see why explaining sacraments apart from the larger ritualed world fails to capture the pervasiveness of rituals in our lives.

Sacraments and liturgies are a subset of our ritualed world. The biblical authors never offer insights into this world focused only on worship services one day a week. At the height of Israel's Temple-centered worship, even animal sacrifices would have involved a pilgrimage of several days, not to mention the preparation of the sacrificial animals, grains, and oils in the months prior to the Temple visit.

In the earliest weekly gatherings of Christians, a distinct feature of the community's worship was the distribution of food to those in need from those with a surplus. In this way the week's abundance for some and the daily poverty of others merged together in the Communion of the saints in worship. ("Saints" just means Jesus-followers.)

Church liturgies don't form the center of our ritualed world, but draw from numerous diverse rituals and routines of the community outside of Sunday routine. Because God creates us as ritualed creatures in community, we can make sense of rites in a workplace, a home, a backyard, a church, a marriage ceremony, and beyond. When we humans do anything, we act, build, plant, pray, and make families in ritual space—wisely or blindly, for good or for ill.

As we've learned, rituals arise from three basic sources. They come from our regular activities, like trying to get out the door on time in the morning. They come from parents, teachers, churches, coaches, and others who prescribe traditions for us to follow. And they come from God and his Son: God prescribed a thick ritualed world for Israel, and Jesus strategically re-tooled those rites for his followers. In every case, there is both guidance and improvisation.

Just think how differently two people practice daily hygiene rituals, how differently two musicians perform a classic piece of music, and how a charismatic worship service differs from a Lutheran service. If we're doing rituals, we're improvising.

Improvising with Ancient Liturgies

Good improvisation comes down to years of practice. Instead of using formal liturgies written out in advance, low church culture tends to favor spontaneity in worship services, especially in the charismatic/Pentecostal circles from which I hail. From my experience pastoring in this context, we may mistake "Spirit-led" worship—which follows a loose structure, with space and toleration for interruptions—with freedom from such formalities. Still, practice informs this worship. Such services aren't usually managed by a printed liturgy for pew sitters to follow. But worshipers can almost predict the exact moments when praise songs will transition to announcements and keep cadence with punctuations of prayer that come and go.

These rhythms draw on "liturgies" in the history of the church, which called for rites such as "benedictions" at the end of each service and "fencing the table" for Communion (i.e., saying who could take the Lord's Supper and under what conditions). Whether aware of it or not, non-denominational charismatic churches now re-appropriate these ancient liturgies, improvising and blending them with American charismatic cultural customs.

Some of these liturgies derive from ancient church practices, some from recent church practices. The charismatic practices of encouraging people to "sing a new song to the Lord," "to go deeper with God," or to "pray to be slain in the Holy Spirit" are all relative newcomers to the liturgy. But gathering to sing hymns, learn from the Scriptures, and receive offerings to benefit the poor goes back more than three thousand years, starting in the times of the Torah.

What Is the Non-Negotiable Basis for Our Ritualed Lives?

The jazz pianist Sir George Shearing reportedly once said, "Learn the rules and then break them in such a way as to exercise good taste." Rules imply rule-makers, whether Harlem jazz greats or prophets appointed by God. When a musician plays jazz, breaking the rules in good taste means showing respect to the roots of the jazz tradition while giving them local and current expression.

Guitar hero Jimi Hendrix rarely played his songs the same way from concert to concert. He sometimes re-arranged entire works between shows. But the songs were always recognizable because he offered his audiences tasteful renditions, which means that he rendered and re-rendered the non-negotiable structures of these songs.

Rituals have instructions but also require improvisation. Although symphony scores leave less room for improvisation, we improvise more heavily in jazz and some forms of stage comedy. But that improvisation requires years of practicing within learned traditions. And in our faith traditions, when we're performing our current expressions of ancient sacraments, certain waypoints help us recognize when we're appropriately practicing rituals or distorting them beyond value.

If we work our way through the Hebrew Bible and the New Testament, some prominent features of ritual show up again and again. We should consider these our guides. The creation stories include three aspects of ritual life: Sabbath, work, and ritual discovery. God rests after creating; God sets the man to work for his benefit; and then God leads the man to discover his wife through the process of naming the animals and not finding a suitable mate. If we ever thought that human embodied action was secondary to our thinking lives, the creation accounts clearly correct us.

Moving further into the Torah, we see the ritual commands of Moses, but also the ritualization of all of life. God gives Israel a myriad of instructions about how to build a house with adequate safety standards, what to do with abused animals, how to treat the trees of their enemies when they go to war, how to practice equity in the marketplace, how to protect people falsely accused of murder and wives accused of adultery, and much more.

When you read through the Torah, I challenge you to name any domain of human activity where the author has not showed Israel that God wants them to care about their practices. On this account, the first Christians would find it bizarre to hear how Christians today sometimes separate their spiritual life from their work and home life.

This emphasis on ritualizing every sphere of life continues into the New Testament as well. Jesus certainly emphasizes that the treatment of people (foreigners, women) and places (marketplace, Temple), and more is part of the spiritual life of Israel. As Abraham Kuyper once famously said, "There is not a square inch in the whole domain of our human existence over which Christ, who is Sovereign over all, does not cry, Mine!"[1]

Accordingly, any attempt we make to improvise the rituals of Scripture must show a profound reverence for Sabbath rest, work for subsistence, the sacrifice of time and money for the sake of others, the communities of God, the immigrant and the poor, the fostering of contentment even in difficult times, and the interconnection of our ethical behavior with everything we do. These are the non-negotiable elements of ritual.

---

1. *Abraham Kuyper: A Centennial Reader*, ed. James D. Bratt (Grand Rapids: Eerdmans, 1998), 488.

Finding Ways to Get the Rites Right

If we've ever looked at the rich history of what Christians have believed and practiced over the centuries, we find a consistent set of habits for understanding Scripture and living it out in both sacred and everyday rituals. Knowing this history can offer us guidance for our practices, helping to steer us toward better rituals within the church. These rituals come with long and principled pedigrees, but they also require improvisation in new contexts.

For instance, we may not ritually scour the streets at night looking for abandoned infants, as the early Roman Christians did. But the principle of caring for the vulnerable and exploited can pervade our believing life today too. We might ritually train people in our church to foster children. Or we might join in the daily and weekly work of helping children who have been functionally abandoned by their families or friends.

The more that Christians have thought about actions like this, the less they tend to think that Scripture alone shows the clear path forward. But Christians have never looked to Scripture alone to determine everything about their ritual practices. Take those earlier examples from the creation story: how do we properly practice Sabbath or perform a wedding ritual strictly according to the Bible? Though both are important rituals in Scripture, the biblical authors don't script them out clearly for us.

So, who gets to write the scripts for us to follow in a wedding according to Scripture alone? What must we do and not do in keeping the Sabbath according to Scripture alone? I'm told by folks in the know that the Protestant Reformation's *sola scriptura* never meant "only and absolutely what Scripture literally says and nothing more." These believers also understood that their Communion practices, weddings, Sabbath habits, and more were forms of improvisation on the principles of the biblical rites.

We might think that the Scriptures script out some rituals down to their minute details while leaving others void of specifics. But Scripture actually doesn't script out any rituals in fine particulars. Like a play or an orchestral score, the script always provides room for improvisation and demands interpretation. Consider these simple questions about biblically scripted rituals:

- Can Communion bread contain cornmeal?
- Which hand do we use to hold the bread of Communion?
- Must we serve wine at communion, or can we use Pepsi?
- What kind of water is required for baptism? Water from a lake, river, or spring?
- Must baptismal water be poured over someone, or must the person be immersed?
- Can we work only five days a week when Scripture commands six days a week? (Does volunteer work count toward working six days a week?)
- Does our work at our job meet the biblical definition of work if it's not physical labor?
- Does cooking on the Sabbath violate the command to rest? If not, then what if we dislike cooking and do it as a service to our children?

While we can't find direct answers to these questions in Scripture, they all can be answered from traditions that root themselves in Scripture. Robin Parry and Andrew Walker, the authors of *Deep Church Rising*, suggest that the church should go deep—back to Scripture itself and to how the church has worked out these questions over time—in order to safely improvise going forward.

We see, for instance, that the church has always valued certain practices in prayer, charity, Scripture reading, and so on. But this doesn't mean that these rites collapse into mindless repetition when they become easily available from ritual habit. Always saying "Amen" at the end of prayers or routinely adding a line item for charitable giving in our budget doesn't necessarily demean the action. And we certainly don't view other areas of life that way.

Also, there are times when rote is what's right. I'm told that air-traffic controllers are trained not to "think on their feet" in an emergency. That might seem counter-intuitive. But because the job requires so many tightly choreographed movements of planes, when something goes wrong, they fall back on a series of rote procedures for the safety of everyone involved. The same goes for pilots.

So it sometimes seems to be with the church. Christianity's interpretations of biblical rituals down through history furrow rote ruts for us to fall into when we need them. We always need to practice discernment, of course, but many of these practices offer safe guidance in tumultuous times, like the rote instructions of air-traffic controllers. And we go forward by reaching back to understand both Scripture and its traditions.

With improvisation currently on the rise, we need to separate in our minds the rituals required across Scripture from the church rituals springing up and cobbled together by local Christians, and then examine these two kinds of rituals closely. Biblical instruction enjoins us to practice Sabbath, Communion, prayer, baptism, and more. It does not command us to sing hymns or tithe ten percent of our paycheck (gross or net). We improvise according to the deep wisdom of the church over time.

Coda

The first command to the man in creation followed a meal ritual: "Eat from all the trees, except that one." The Crucifixion, the central drama of Christianity, enacted a sacrificial ritual. Christians gathered in churches today perform a ritual meal based on Jesus's sacrifice. The final scene of the new heavens and new earth depict the ritual participation of all people in the New Jerusalem. Clearly our cosmos has been ritualed from the beginning and will be to the end. The explorations in these chapters have been our ritual attempts to reflect on the implications of that simple truth.

The ritual of book reading now nears completion between us. Given what we understand from Scripture and the rest of our world, what do we do now? One thing is certain: we can't afford to have a simplistic view of our ritualed world. We now know— whether we've paid attention to it or not—that we perform rituals according to scripts in every area of our lives.

And if the reading rite did its job, then perhaps we'll see rituals differently, maybe even more clearly. We'll take a careful inventory of our own lives. We'll search out the essential rites in Scripture and do them! Knowing the tenets of our ritualed lives, we'll take care to improvise according to the kind of good taste that respects tradition.

In this world of competing rituals, God seems to want us to do particular things with our hearts, minds, and bodies in our communities in particular times and circumstances. These essential rites, shaped over the centuries, are worth our sustained reflection and embodiment. Wax on, wax off.

Appendix

Examples of a Ritual Inventory

As the American football coach Vince Lombardi used to say to his players, "Gentlemen, this is a football."[1] In other words, we need to start from scratch. I don't do sports, so don't worry—that's the full extent of my athletic illustrations. Allow me to mix the metaphor. If the ship is listing because of shifted cargo, then righting the ship involves locating the problem and fixing it.

Up to now, we've been finding the scattered cargo of ritual life. Now we need to lock it back down in its proper places. To straighten the teetering ship, we need to start again with Lombardi-like resolve. "Ladies and gentlemen, this is a ritual."

I know that as I'm writing (and you're reading) this, you and I have been reassessing many of our rituals at home, work, and church. I feel especially concerned that you'll want checklists or a list of "dos" and "don'ts." Or you'll want me to address something close to what you face in your daily lives. But I don't have the moral imagination to think up every way in which this reassessment affects you and me.

I can only share with you what has been shared with me and what I've discovered in practice. Please understand that above all

---

1. Thanks to Gregory Thornbury for reminding me of this saying.

my suggestions stands a large banner that reads, "What I Think I've Learned . . . Probably."

Caveat Scriptor

To make the point more pretentiously, I'm using the Latin phrase *caveat scriptor* ("Let the writer beware"). I've said it several times now, but I'll say it again: the biblical authors presume that we understand why we perform these rituals and expect us to be able to explain them to our children.

And we're all scripting rituals for others, whether for children or peers or co-workers. As we know now, we should be careful about what we prescribe. Because embodying rites costs time and energy, we might think of it as an economic concern, but that's not what I'm worried about.

My concern is that bad rituals can be created, much of the time unwittingly. In a ritual-eat-ritual world, dark and flimsy rites can win out over healthy rituals. All the more reason that we can't afford to take the view that we don't play in the game of rites. We need to be good at the fundamentals, recognizing how healthy rites have always shaped our thriving in the world. And with a solid grasp of the basics, we can safely improvise and flourish.

"Ladies and gentlemen, these are some of my rituals."

My Ritual Inventory

To assess my ritualed world in an inventory, I'll ask myself the following questions about my practices:

1. Who prescribes it?
2. To what end?

3. How do I/we safely improvise it?
4. How can this ritual turn dark or flimsy?
5. Reflections/response?

Ritual: Buying up-to-date outfits for work

Who prescribes it?

Me and my culture: I want to be seen a certain way in my work environment. Clothing manufacturers who've understood my desires have made and advertised particular clothes suited to my goals. And cultural standards for work clothes and current fashions/styles have influenced my ritual.

To what end?

I want to be perceived in a particular way by clients, co-workers, and management. I want to feel good about the way I look (as interpreted to me by cultural standards and clothing manufacturers). I also want to satisfy my current desire to shop and buy new things.

How do I safely improvise it?

By setting an annual clothing budget and sticking to it. By thinking about the need for new clothes and the mere desire for them. By examining the source of my sense of "having enough" and setting a "having enough" threshold for clothing. By examining why I like to shop and/or buy new things and how that affects budgeting and purchasing decisions.

How can this ritual turn dark or flimsy?

When unplanned spending violates my budget boundaries. When I engage in habitual, addiction-like purchasing or become obsessed with online shopping. When I feel dissatisfied with recent purchases, only able to appreciate "the next buy."

Reflections

If the ritual is becoming obsessive (dark), I might be finding too much of my identity in transient and vain ways. I have to wear something, but it might be that I'm becoming ritualized into a life centered on what I wear and how I buy it. This could be dangerous.

Ritual: Playing Candy Crush at bedtime (a simple pattern-finding game)

Who prescribes it?

Me and game designers

To what end?

Candy Crush is made for mindless entertainment. After the dozens of conversations and pressing tasks of the day, I use this to distract myself at the end of the night. Essentially, it "unwinds" me from the day's fervor.

How do I safely improvise it?

This game has no internal features that would make me want to stop playing it (see below). But it does make me sleepy, and often I can't finish a full round of the game before putting my computer down and falling asleep.

How can this ritual turn dark or flimsy?

If I didn't set time limits for this game, it could become addictive and cause me to play at work or at other times when I should be doing something else. If I played on a smartphone, it could interfere with my sleep hygiene. (Having a smartphone near my bed isn't conducive to slumber.)

Reflections

I need to be careful with what I use to unwind at night. This practice could hinder sleep or get used as a tool to ignore people or problems.

Ritual: Walking to church on Sundays (about 1.5 miles)

Who prescribes it?

My wife and I

To what end?

To get some exercise, enjoy some family time, clear our minds before church, keep in touch with the neighborhood, etc.

How do we safely improvise it?

We walk when the weather isn't brutally hot or cold. Insisting that we walk regardless of weather or health could defeat the goal, especially for our kids. Discernment is required every Sunday morning.

How can this ritual turn dark or flimsy?

If we walked without using the time to talk with each other, this would be a "thin rite."

Reflections

I like this ritual, and I know my kids might complain about it occasionally, but they'll eventually look back on it fondly.

Ritual: Regular—but not daily—Scripture reading

Who prescribes it?

It's never prescribed, but implied to be a necessary part of a God-directed life by Scripture itself (Deut. 17:18; Ps. 1:1–2; 111:2; Ezra 7:10; Neh. 8:1–8; Matt. 21:42; Luke 10:26; Acts 8:28; etc.).

To what end?

To understand the content and nature of the Bible as literature. To understand what God has spoken (and what God hasn't spoken) through the prophets. To know who God is and what God is up to in the world around me.

How do I safely improvise it?

Reading to understand means that I can't read a verse or a passage at a time and out of context. I have to read big chunks or entire books at a time. I avoid reading small passages or verses at a time.

How can this ritual turn dark or flimsy?

Dark: Treating the words of Scripture as if they were magical or worshiping the Bible itself.

Flimsy: Not having a robust enough understanding of the biblical authors and what they've said so that I blindly or naively repeat verses or concepts from Scripture out of context. (I worry that daily devotional reading models can sometimes transform into dark and/or flimsy rituals.)

Reflections

I like to use various Scripture reading schedules and programs, but I tend to go too long without deep reading because it's not a daily habit. Some people might need daily reading to keep them engaged.

Ritual: Sabbath: No electronics or screens from sundown Friday to sundown Saturday

Who prescribes it?

There is a biblical basis for this, but in this form, my wife and I prescribe it.

To what end?

To encourage taking extended time away from electronics and to force boredom, which leads to productive time-keeping. To encourage a healthy distancing from our electronic products.

How do we safely improvise it?

We can all choose to watch a movie together as an exception to the no-screen rule.

How can this ritual turn dark or flimsy?

My wife and I have noticed that this practice can foster a certain loathing for our kids' electronic habits; we also realize that this Sabbath fast from screens feels self-righteously good to the two of us. We want our kids to see these devices as tools, but to be cautious with them. Practicing this ritual overzealously could backfire on that front.

Reflections

I like this ritual, although we don't practice it consistently. And I know my kids might complain about it occasionally, but they'll eventually look back on it fondly.

Your Ritual Inventory

Now it's your turn. Below I've listed some areas in our lives that we should all inventory.

Ritual: Shopping Ritual

Who prescribes it?

To what end?

How do I/we safely improvise it?

How can this ritual turn dark or flimsy?

Reflections/response?

Ritual: Weekend Ritual

Who prescribes it?

To what end?

How do I/we safely improvise it?

How can this ritual turn dark or flimsy?

Reflections/response?

Ritual: Smartphone Use

Who prescribes it?

To what end?

How do I/we safely improvise it?

How can this ritual turn dark or flimsy?

Reflections/response?

Ritual: Relationship Maintenance Ritual

Who prescribes it?

To what end?

How do I/we safely improvise it?

How can this ritual turn dark or flimsy?

Reflections/response?

Ritual: Education/Learning Ritual

Who prescribes it?

To what end?

How do I/we safely improvise it?

How can this ritual turn dark or flimsy?

Reflections/response?

Ritual: Media Consumption Ritual

Who prescribes it?

To what end?

How do I/we safely improvise it?

How can this ritual turn dark or flimsy?

Reflections/response?

Suggested Reading

If you want the extended academic argument behind this book, see my monograph *Knowledge by Ritual: A Biblical Prolegomenon to Sacramental Theology* (Eisenbrauns, 2016).

On Christian Life Rituals

- *Essential Worship: A Handbook for Leaders* by Greg Scheer. Baker Books, 2016.
- *The Liturgy of Death* by Alexander Schmemann. St. Vladimir's Seminary Press, 2017.
- *Liturgy of the Ordinary: Sacred Practices in Everyday Life* by Tish Harrison Warren. InterVarsity Press, 2016.
- *Naked and Unashamed: A Guide to the Necessary Work of Christian Marriage* by Jerry Root, Claudia Root, and Jeremy Rios. Paraclete Press, 2018.
- *Practicing the King's Economy: Honoring Jesus in How We Work, Earn, Spend, Save, and Give* by Michael Rhodes, Robby Holt, and Brian Fikkert. Baker Books, 2018.

On Practical Matters

- *Alone Together: Why We Expect More from Technology and Less from Each Other* by Sherry Turkle. Basic Books, 2017. (Anything by Sherry Turkle will be good!)
- *The Body Keeps the Score: Brain, Mind, and Body in the Healing of Trauma* by Bessel van der Kolk. Penguin Books, 2015.
- *Irresistible: The Rise of Addictive Technology and the Business of Keeping Us Hooked* by Adam Alter. Penguin Books, 2018.
- *A Little Manual for Knowing* by Esther Lightcap Meek. Cascade, 2014.